DRI

DREADLOCKS

LES ISAAC
with Alistair Forrest

Marshalls

Marshalls Paperbacks
Marshall Morgan & Scott
3 Beggarwood Lane, Basingstoke, Hants., UK.

First published by Marshall Morgan & Scott 1984

ISBN 0 551 01097 5

Printed in Great Britain by
Hunt Barnard Printing Ltd., Aylesbury, Bucks.

Contents

Foreword

I'd had enough. My dad had pushed me once too often. I slammed the door behind me and walked out into the morning to buy a machete. But God wanted more from my life than life imprisonment for murder – he wanted to set me free to be a witness to the power to change a life. He intervened to change me from a Rasta into an evangelist for Jesus Christ. It is this journey that I recall in this book.

I write this book so non-Christians can realise the power of God to transform lives. In particular I address myself to young blacks and Rastas. In this book I aim to show the greater hope and purpose to be found in Jesus Christ, the Son of God. He met my greatest need – not to find my roots, or my culture – but my soul's need of forgiveness and love, and something 'real' to live for.

I write this book also for Christians. I include snap shots of my life after conversion, and growth with Christ living out his life through me. The message here is that we *can* do all things through Christ who strengthens us. God can transform and then go on to work through *anyone*'s life the way that he is doing through mine.

My highest praise and thanks is to the Lord Jesus Christ who has made all this possible, who has indeed worked through people mentioned in this book like Davison, sister Gwen, my pastor David Perry, pastor Franklin (and many others) who did so much to encourage me in my early Christian experience.

I acknowledge also the way that God has brought me into fellowship with people like Andrew and Pauline Brandon, who share with me a similar vision for the salvation of many souls through our ministry together.

My heart's praise to God, finally, is for my wife Louise who has been a continuous support and inspiration since our marriage three years ago, in my ministry and in writing this book.

I believe that this is just the beginning of God's work in my life. My mission continues and my love for Christ grows stronger. My prayer for you is that you will know Christ and be encouraged and challenged as you read this book.

1: The promised land

The faces stared relentlessly. Fat ones, thin ones, round ones, young ones, old ones. And all white faces.

'So this is England,' I thought, blinking my seven-year-old unbelieving eyes at the sea of white people at the airport. It was Heathrow, March 1965. The Isaac children were four little black faces amid all the white ones, and we were strangers.

I half ran, stumbling as I tripped over my untied shoelaces, after my older sister Lemina who, at the grand age of ten, had decided she was our leader. We didn't quarrel.

The four of us hustled past the white faces, not really knowing where we were going, but sure that just following everybody else was good enough. The white faces could not have known the significance of one of the four little black faces. But when I look back at the fading memories, I realise with gratitude that the BAC 1-11 that had just flown in from Antigua had brought one of God's special packages.

If you had just touched down on a flight from the North Pole and were sampling for the first time the bright sunshine that had taken over from a dull cold and wet winter, you might be tempted to stay purely for the weather. But the four of us – Lemina, Vernon, Cynthia and me – had only hours before been in the sweltering coconut and sugarcane climate of the West Indies, and England's March felt more like Antarctica's January.

Wide-eyed, we looked around without a murmur. Only Lemina seemed in any way agitated, feeling obliged to touch each one of us in turn, as if to make sure we were all still there. We were looking for our parents, whom we had not seen for a few years. In fact, I had no idea what they looked like. I knew I would know them when we found them, or they found us, but I couldn't conjure up a mental picture of them.

Our parents found us huddled together near the customs desks, and interrupted my aimlessly wandering dream into which I had lapsed as I studied more of the strange white faces. My father, Enoch Isaac, seemed big to me. But I suppose it was more that I was so small, because it was stockiness rather than height that gave him an appearance of bulkiness. He looked at me with cold eyes, but just a hint of a smile made me feel secure as he picked me up and gave me a rib-crushing squeeze.

My mother, Victoria, was darker skinned than my father, and just her colour made me feel more at home. She was in her twenties, quite a few years younger than my father who was well into his thirties, and she was well built and fit-looking. She chuckled and gurgled as she hugged us each in turn, planting a damp kiss on my forehead and repeating my name over and over again.

We were hustled out of the airport and into a waiting car. I spent almost the entire trip staring wide-eyed out of the window, taking in the suburban scenes of London, the giant city that was just getting into full swing in the swinging sixties. To me, it was the land of milk and honey, subject of so many bedtime stories, but the stories hadn't told me of the sprawling bricks and concrete which formed a totally new concept for me. But here was the ultimate dream being realised. The ambition of every child back home in John Hughes village—to be in England.

I went back to thinking about my parents. I had experienced that complete shock to the system when people you have thought about for so long turn out to be different from the way you imagined them. They had left us in the care of our grandmother in John Hughes village some four years previously, just long enough for their memory to have faded in our young minds.

The sudden shock of seeing them again had taken me by surprise, and strangely subdued me. Normally I was capable of generating enough energy for twenty children of my age, but on this occasion I had become reflective and rather quiet. But now, in the back seat of the Cortina belonging to a friend of the family, I dragged my gaze from the roadside scenes and looked from my mother to my father and at last caught the reality of the occasion. I was home.

The cramped Islington basement flat contrasted starkly with the large, rambling house in John Hughes village, instantly bringing a rush of new fears to me. How could the four of us, so used to running barefoot from the house to play on the beach, get accustomed to this dark, damp flat? In later weeks, as the driving rain sent torrents running down the steps and brought ugly green and black damp patches to the walls, I would close my eyes and try to cling to the fading memories of my calypso sunshine island.

I had been taught by my grandmother to get up with the dawn to take the donkey and several goats to their scrawny pasture. Then, with the other children, I would race back home for a quick breakfast before school. There a caning awaited any unfortunate child who in haste has not combed their hair properly, for the head teacher ran a pencil through each curly black head looking for tangles and knots. Finger-nails had to be spotless. Clothes – well, at least clean, if not exactly the latest school uniform from Harrods.

A big change in lifestyle I soon noticed was the way I was no longer taking my life in my hands when I met an adult on the street. In Antigua, passing the time of day with your elder was not a rule to be neglected but, to my amazement, nobody in this strange country seemed to talk to one another. I even tried pulling faces at several adults and, quite to my surprise, I was ignored!

I missed the simple way of life, the ramshackle fishing boats, tatty straw hats and the old beggar in my neighbourhood who would shout to me, 'Hey, kid, ya got any mangoes, boy?' I let the memories fade. As consciously as a child of my age could, I determined to make the most of this green land of fair-haired strangers, and there and then decided the sheer enormity of the place would not overwhelm me, and Les Isaac would never be second to anyone. And even then, the seething aggression began to well up in me, even before my first real encounter with racial prejudice and my first bruising from the white boy's fists.

Alfred Pritchard School was a big Victorian building. Roman Catholic downstairs, C of E upstairs, and attended by an increasing number of little black children from the West Indies. As soon as our mother left us for our first day, Vernon and I were being called 'golliwogs' by other white children. 'What's a golliwog?' I asked my older brother. I didn't get a response because Vernon didn't know either. We found out one teatime while studying the jar of jam.

Each day at school brought a new awareness that we were classed as different creatures, and one of the first big words I learned was 'prejudice'.

One day I found myself surrounded by four white boys in the playground. 'Hey, golliwog,' they snarled, and the sudden awareness that this was more than name-calling came over me. One of them came close enough to let a fast right jab fly, my head jerked painfully back, and red blood trickled from my nose. That was the moment when I really discovered my temper, and my strength. As the four of them lashed out together, I grabbed the first object that came to hand – a rounders bat. I had time to lay out one of my attackers before a teacher waded into the mêlée and gripped me by the ear. She held my ear so tightly I screamed out in pain, kicking and struggling. And while she held me, the four attackers continued to punch and kick at me, and spit on me, and she did nothing to stop them.

I learned fast that I was hated by many because of my skin, and people would take advantage of me whenever they could. I made friends with other West Indian children, and the white boys quickly became less friendly and often the enemy. And I soon learned how to hate.

2: Clenched fists

'Les, I need some potatoes, git yoursel' to the shop for me!' I always obeyed my mother. I took the shopping bag from her, and dashed out of the front door into the street.

As I neared the corner shop, the pavement was blocked by four tough-looking white youths. I thought about turning to run and, looking over my shoulder, with a certain amount of relief saw Vernon sprinting to my side.

One of the youths slowly took off his belt, and as he swung it around his head he snarled, 'Come and get it, nigger boys.' Vernon took a step forward. The youth hesitated, having expected both of us to make a break for it, and then he swiped at Vernon with the belt. Vernon held out his arm, the belt wrapped itself around it harmlessly, and the weapon was wrenched viciously from the youth's hands. Encouraged by this success, the two of us pitched in, with flying arms and fists, and within seconds the four boys turned and ran.

White men to me had always been Americans and the occasional Englishman back home in Antigua, never looking for a fight unless very drunk, and then only prepared to swing a fist if it meant there would be more rum as a result. Naked aggression like this was unexpected, and a growing nightmare.

I lay on my bed and tried out those fading dreams again. The memory of the big white evangelist came back, but only those parts that had some peculiarity about them. I remembered the big American's shabby white suit, the enormous sweat stains under and around his shoulders, and the sweatdrops running off his nose while he preached. I remembered quite vividly the fat cigar the bulky missionary puffed throughout his sermon without removing it once, and how I had spent much of the time wondering how a man could talk with a thing that size in his mouth.

Yes, I could also remember singing 'Blessed assurance, Jesus is mine.' The hundred or so people at the open-air meeting that day had sung it at least three times, I recalled. What was that sermon about? Something about Jesus loving everybody, and that people belonged to him. I had a picture of Jesus, and I could also clearly remember that this Jesus was white. Could it be that white people with their white Jesus could hate black people and want to hurt them? And why wasn't there a black Jesus to help people like me?

In the sixties black ghettos sprang up all over North London, not to mention Wolverhampton and Bradford. But when I was ten my family moved to a large housing estate in Camden where each of us was as conspicuous as if we had sported two heads. We were the first black family to move in.

Refusing to be bullied, Vernon and I made friends with most of the kids of our age on the estate. For a short time it was almost as if colour didn't matter anymore. But the dream was shattered on the many occasions when older boys either moved in or passed through, disrupting friendly soccer games and neighbourhood larks with their taunts of 'nigger' and 'wog'.

To me, the local church near the estate was a breeding ground for the attitudes that made me a victim. It was a white man's church. Suspicious looks from prim and proper church-goers wearing their Sunday best just made me feel God was not interested in West Indians. And they talked another language, especially the minister in his flowing robes, that I could not understand.

I was there because of my parents' compulsive sense of religious duty. The whole family had to go every week. It seemed like the weekly highlight was wrenching off my tie, after getting out of church, like the fizz exploding from a shaken bottle. Tearing off my jacket in a frantic effort to look scruffy like my friends, I would somehow be racing my brother to see who could get dirtiest quickest before Sunday lunch.

Vernon had been a year at Archway Secondary School in the heart of Islington when we both change schools and I joined him at the age of eleven. It was a world of bigger white boys with mean hearts, most of them with very different ideas except in the realm of discrimination. Resplendent in my new blazer, neat tie and smart trousers, I was a prime target for any aggro that was going.

The 'softy boys' cowered at one end of the playground. The 'bad boys' dragged heavily on their cigarettes at the other, noticeable with their heavy boots and turned-up Levi's. I wasn't sure at which end I belonged, but I seemed to be drawn to the mean end.

On that very first day a bully boy picked on a softy much smaller than himself. As if unaware of the unwritten rules, I intervened.

'Hey mate, wotcha doing? Leave that guy alone,' I said. Silence. Then the bad boy growled, 'Who are you? You offerin' me out?'

I knew that to be the challenge of 'Come outside and get what's coming to you', and my next words surprised me as I spoke them. 'Yeah, I'll meet you after school.' When Vernon heard about it, he was equally shocked, and very worried.

By the time the bell rang out to end the last lesson, word had gone around the entire school that there would be a fight involving a new boy, who happened to be a West Indian, and a white bully. As I came out through the main gate there was a large crowd yelling 'knuckle' over and over again. There in the centre of the crowd was my opponent.

There were no formalities. I didn't even see the right hook coming, and it split my lip. The pain seared through my mouth, and I felt the hot blood run down my chin.

Fury boiled up in me immediately. I flew at the white boy, fists flailing, and we fell heavily to the ground. The white boy grunted, and almost at the same time a friend of Vernon's put the boot in and the fight was as good as over. The white boy was unconscious. I was pulled off, not knowing whether to be grateful or disappointed. Seconds later my defeated opponent, looking distinctly wobbly in the legs, staggered away crying.

Word spread through the school that Les Isaac was tough, a new champ, but deep down I knew I had only won with unfair assistance from my brother's friend. In the following weeks I got a reputation as one of the best fighters in the school, second only to the unquestioned hard boys who ruled the roost.

3: The geezers

The child spat. He was not yet in his teens, yet he mimicked the skinheads of his day. Hands in his pockets, skuffing his heavy black boots on the playground tarmac, his cigarette hanging loosely from his thin, mean lips, the boy spoke with his fellow 'geezers' about how many girlfriends he had.

Martin's father had set up a shop in London, selling sweets and cigarettes. That gave him a quick route to popularity with the likes of me and the other playground toughs, for he stole cigarettes from his father's shop. His speciality was fat Winston Churchill cigars which the hardest boys puffed to show who was in charge.

Today he chatted with his friends. One of them was Kostos, the son of a Greek businessman. Outwardly, Kostos had the appearance of being a 'softy' – always well dressed, clean, and with combed hair. But inside Kostos could hold his own with the meanest. He was a rebel. His eleven years of conforming to the outward appearance of being happy with his wealthy background had welled up and now he had found company to give his fake life some meaning. Kostos held on to his suave appearance and his parents thought he was an angel, but they could not see inside.

The third of my set of close friends was David, dark hair neatly combed, striking good looks, his quiet way helping to give him the appearance of being older than the others.

Just then, I sauntered up. 'Give us a lug,' I said to Martin, holding out my hand expecting the cigarette to be passed to me. Martin inhaled deeply, and obliged. The four of us were gradually being drawn together and frequently we stood by each other in neighbourhood skirmishes.

The plan was simple. There were three registration times in

each school day, supervized by a tutorial teacher. Martin, David and Kostos and I would always sign on at the morning tutorial, but whether we actually registered at lunchtime and at four o'clock depended on how much fun we were having about town. We didn't think much of attending classes.

Sometimes Lemina would write me a fabricated note excusing me from school, for my mother was always too busy at work to keep tabs on us children.

A regular morning jaunt was a trip to Regent's Park and London Zoo. Lunch was invariably at a café with enough pinball machines to keep the four of us happy. And afternoons were usually spent at the cinema – but not via the front entrance, for we had learnt how to open fire exits from the outside.

This would last for a week or two weeks at a time. Then we'd have a period at school, just to make sure our faces were seen.

'Heads', the squeaky voices screamed. Their heads bobbing with excitement, the seven kneeling boys had found a wide section of corridor for their 'heads and tails' mini-gambling fling. They huddled as the coin was flipped again, each one hoping that today was that day with a little bit of extra luck. They were so engrossed, they didn't see us – the mean four – turn the corner, spot the game and move in for easy pickings.

I kicked the nearest youngster aside. As the boy squealed and ran, Martin rough-handled the rest while Kostos scooped up the pennies and sixpenny pieces. Shoving the coins into his pockets, while David and I cleaned up behind him, the four of us bolted and within seconds the robbery was complete.

The small bands of children soon learned from this thuggish behaviour and appointed look-outs who gave them the word when my cronies and I came on the scene.

As the steady flow of cash from busted gambling circles started to dry up, we dreamed up new evil enterprises. Our favourite was a kind of protection racket which meant finding an unsuspecting child on his own somewhere and persuading him he wanted to part with some change. A lot depended on whether my mother had won at bingo, for if she had I was better looked after in terms of cash hand-outs and wasn't so desperate. But if she hadn't, I was usually short and consequently took it out on a suitably feeble junior. A good day would bring in £1 or more.

Then there was the dinner ticket racket. David, Martin, Kostos and I had suppliers – children entitled to free meals who chose to go home instead. The tickets were duly handed over to we young sharks who could make clear profit on each one by selling them to other children.

One day the four of us, having arranged our usual bunk from school, headed for Kostos's home. It was a comfortable house by North London standards, pleasantly large and very well furnished. Kostos's parents both worked, so the house was empty.

Kostos let us in. We made ourselves at home, lighting cigarettes as we lounged in the easy chairs. Kostos got up, crossed the living-room floor, and opened up the drinks cabinet.

'I'll have a scotch,' I said. A generous measure was sloshed into an expensive whisky glass.

Martin joked, 'Bring me a brandy, boy' and Kostos poured two beers for him and David, knowing that was what they really wanted.

Much conversation followed, most of it superfluous, except for the odd remark like, 'We're broke' or 'Where can we get some cash?' The drift of the chatter was that somewhere in the house there had to be some source of supply that firstly, shouldn't be missed, and secondly, wouldn't really be needed by such a successful businessman as Kostos's father.

That line of thought led us to two sources. The gas and electricity meters. It was while forcing these open that David found a new method of securing a regular income: every telephone box in the district contained a cash box waiting to be raided. And if anyone had the knack of relieving the Post Office of its shillings, it was David.

The skinhead cult was now in full swing, and my three

chums and I were hooked. Most of them were white, hair cropped minutely short or even shaved off completely, but some were black. However, I did not feel out of place, neither was I considered unusual by white skinheads.

Our gear was distinct, Harrington jackets, Ben Sherman shirts, staypress mod trousers or Levi jeans turned up at the ankle, and heavy Dr Martin boots. My small set looked hard and mean, but we were also well dressed, never sloppy. We aimed to 'pull the birds' as well as frighten off the opposition.

I grew accustomed to walking around with my right hand permanently in my jacket pocket, fingering the lethal flick-knife I had taken to carrying at all times. It nearly landed me in court, for although I had a masterful knack of avoiding the law at crucial moments, I went close to throwing away my freedom on numerous occasions.

One escape from the clutches of the law, which was frankly inexplicable, was during a school outing. It was a dull, rainy afternoon, and perhaps it was the gloom that had persuaded me I should actually spend the day at school. The entire class was taken to an art gallery, in an attempt to inspire a greater degree of creativity in the likes of Les Isaac.

Hands in pockets, and missing my pals, I shuffled round the gallery with the rest of the class, with only the teacher and his enthusiastic 'pets' getting excited about what I considered to be pretty average art. I never found landscapes captivating: why not gaze at the real thing if you enjoy it, I would argue.

However, when at the end of the tour some watercolour paintings were being handed out to any of the pupils who wanted them, I changed my mind. I saw one that would go nicely on my bedroom wall, but as soon as my eyes alighted on it so did the gaze of a tall, tough-looking boy whom I had never really got to know. Both of us reached out simultaneously for the painting.

'Push off,' I snarled, expecting the youth to back off instantly.

Either he was not aware of my reputation, stupid, or just unafraid, for the youth's cool blue eyes calmly held my gaze.

'I'm not frightened of you, rastus,' he said quietly.

That word made something snap inside me. My eyes flashed, and my right hand flew from my pocket, making that ominous click with the frightening flash of silver.

The youth hit out in defence catching me across the cheek. My left arm jabbed out, and the youth was so busy watching the darting blade he didn't see the other blow coming. I caught him savagely in the mouth and he was momentarily stunned. That let me in to throw my left arm around the youth's neck; I drew him tight, and without stopping to think of the consequences my knife hand found that soft spot just below the rib cage.

All this happened in a flash. The other children in the class all drew back in fear, and someone shouted 'He's got a knife, he's got a knife', just as a red stain appeared on the youth's white shirt just above his trousers.

If the teacher hadn't forced his way between us, I might have seriously wounded the youth. As it was, I inflicted two superficial cuts, although serious enough to merit long discussions by senior staff at the school about the possibility of bringing in the police. As it was, I even got off without being expelled from school, and how that happened I could not work out.

Was I lucky? My class mates said so. Or would it have been better for a magistrate to have attempted to stop my reckless life going on in its downward direction? If that had happened, the terrifying violence that was to etch deep emotions into my life might not have occurred, but neither would the deep spiritual reaction that ultimately resulted.

4: The crew fight

I steadily made friends with a whole new set with whom I mixed as soon as school was over. Again they were all white – Bernie, Jonjo, Tom, Mark, Tony, Pat – but we were all good friends who spent time together and stood up for one another.

We frequented clubs and cafés in the Islington area, preferably joints where there was an abundance of pinball machines or table soccer. And our transport was invariably stolen scooters or, if not enough could be found and nicked, then it was a case of jumping barriers and pushing past ticket collectors at tube stations.

Bernie was a good friend of mine in the days of visiting these wayward joints, even though he didn't look the skinhead type with his gold-rimmed spectacles and rare mop of tousled hair. But he was by far the best pinball player.

One night Bernie, two others and I were on our own at a youth club playing the machines. The club was fuller than usual because there were a number of youths there from Finchley, laughing and joking with each other and showing off in front of their 'birds'.

I left Bernie clocking up his inevitable thousands of points while I went to the gents. When I came out I immediately saw something that spelled trouble. One of the Finchley skinheads was leaning on Bernie's pinball machine, showing off to his denimed girlfriend by baiting my bespectacled friend. Bernie was clearly agitated. When he reacted because his vision of the table was obscured, the Finchley boy rounded on him.

'You eyin' my girl' he accused Bernie.

I knew there was trouble brewing, because a statement like that was really an open challenge for a fight. Just then the two other youths with us sauntered over and stood staring at the Finchley boy.

The youth hit Bernie hard in the mouth, and his specs clattered to the floor. The crowded club suddenly fell silent, and all heads turned towards us. Bernie wanted to calm the youth down because he didn't much like fighting, and meanwhile I had quickly realised that to retaliate would be suicidal as most of the youths in the youth club would probably side with the Finchley boy.

I leapt into the few feet of space between the two of them as Bernie reached for his specs. I appeared older than my thirteen years and the sight of a muscular black youth, eyes showing no hint of fear, made the aggressor hesitate. The split-second opportunity was there and, with the signal from me, we made a dash for the door.

The blast of cold air on our faces was welcome as we bolted into the street, for we realised we were on a hiding to nothing if we stayed put. We ran hard, Bernie's lip bleeding profusely and smarting with pain, until we realised we were not being chased. Then we made for home to look for our friends and consolation.

Talking about it with our mates meant it wasn't long before the general consensus of opinion was that revenge was the only possible course of action. By the next evening we had recruited fifty youths to go and look for the culprit, and most likely pitch into a crew-fight, Archway versus Finchley. Among the most noticeable of our newly formed gang was Errol, stocky, muscular and jet black, with a clenched fist of iron the size of a pint beer mug. At eighteen, he was one of the oldest, and years of prejudice against his colour had bred an untamed aggression that had brought quite a reputation for the feared lad from Islington.

We made our way to Finchley and roamed the streets around the youth club looking for the youth who had so cruelly struck Bernie. No success. Frustration began to build up, and I feared that if we didn't find our quarry soon the crew would begin to drift apart. Hungry for action, one youth pitched a brick through the youth club's window, and suddenly the entire fifty of us ran as if expecting the police to burst instantly on the scene. As we rushed round a corner into Finchley High Road, Errol and I, who were in the lead, came to a sudden halt. There, only about 50 yards away, were what could only be described as 'real geezers'. Five of them. Dressed immaculately in crombies and Gatsby hats, even carrying what appeared to be violin cases. They must all be mates of the youth, I thought.

'These must be friends of the guy,' I shouted, 'let's give 'em a kickin.' My rabble-rousing call was all that was needed for our Archway mob to go into action, particularly Errol. With a blood-curdling war-cry, he led the field as the five geezers turned and saw for the first time the incredible odds they had to face.

Traffic came to a halt. Petrified drivers wound up their windows and locked their doors. Several cars had their windscreens smashed by bicycle chains or axe handles as we ran past, and shop windows were shattered. The five geezers stood no chance, and they were lucky to be left alive, though they put up a brave fight considering the odds that were stacked against them.

In the few minutes before the police arrived, Finchley High Road was devastated, mainly because it was 'enemy' territory, but also because the fifty of us could not all get at five opponents at one time, and the naked aggression had to be turned on to something vulnerable. As the sirens approached we all ran, for we knew good escape routes that had been previously agreed, but I was the last to leave, shouting over my shoulder 'We'll be back on Wednesday. Be ready this time'.

The brawl had worked up quite a steady flow of adrenalin in each of us, and on our way back we paid a visit to a sweet shop owned by an Asian man in his fifties.

'Don't move a muscle or we'll give you a kickin',' I announced as I sauntered in with three boys. The Asian, staring at us with wide eyes as we filled the doorway, duly obeyed. Half-a-dozen of us helped ourselves to ice-creams and sweets while the shop-keeper cowered in a corner. I felt as though I could do anything, and I was king in my own domain. But when I later reflected on the evening's work, having again beaten the police by using a prearranged escape route, I suddenly felt empty. All we had done was outnumber some skinhads ten to one and rob a very frightened Asian. Big deal. Wednesday would be better. It had to be.

During the next few days Errol, Bernie and I recruited about 200 youths by announcing there was to be a crew-fight against Finchley skins. And it was some rabble, varying in age from twelve to nineteen, some carrying hammers, some chains and some nursing lethal machetes. Almost all of us had knives.

At school, I had a brainwave during a chemistry lesson. My class was doing an experiment with acid, and while the teacher was writing on the blackboard, I poured nitric acid into a container, screwed on the cap, and popped it into my blazer breast pocket. I could imagine the Finchley enemy screaming in pain with burning faces.

The next class was religious education. Midway through a most boring lesson on the ethics of war, I noticed a strange vapour coming from my jacket, and my chest was irritatingly itchy. I pulled my jacket open to see a gaping, ragged hole not only through the blazer's lining but also through my shirt, and beneath it my skin was peeling.

I thrust the container into my desk, made the inevitable excuse and was allowed, albeit with glowering looks from the teacher, to go to the toilet. The moment I was in the corridor, I broke into a sprint and on arrival at the boy's washroom tore off my blazer, shirt and tie, and splashed cold water on my peeling skin.

Meanwhile, as the class ended, one of my classmates brought the container, and despite the curt order to get rid of the lethal acid, it was brought into technical drawing, where it caused even more havoc.

My friend lasted just ten minutes in that lesson before his agonised scream brought teacher and pupils running over to him. While the teacher puzzled over the holes burned into the screaming boy's side, I stealthily snatched up the container and hid it in an unattended desk.

The boy was rushed to hospital to be treated for burns, and I threw the acid down a drain. Even to a hardened West Indian like me, who had seen many a savage fight, this weapon was too horrible and too cowardly to be used on even the skinhead who had hit Bernie.

The small army that gathered at Archway that Wednesday was full of pent-up frustration. Only a handful of us were actually looking for revenge, and in the rest there were varying reactions to parents, society, police and people in general that were about to erupt in violence. And in a few there was just that sheepish instinct to follow the crowd.

The first thing the ticket inspector at Finchley station knew about that evening's crew-fight was the sound of 400 Dr Martins boots drumming on the metal staircase. It was a terrifying sound. He just stared open mouthed, not even daring to hold out his hand for tickets for fear of having it chopped off by one of the ugly machetes he saw being brandished. And for many minutes after the last of us had jogged past, he just sat there bewildered, and made that strange decision that people can never explain afterwards. He didn't tell anyone. Not the local inspector, not the underground headquarters, not the police.

We turned a corner and came face to face with the enemy. No searching on this occasion for the beaten-up youths had made sure the enemy would be prepared this time, and they were waiting. A quick estimate showed me that Archway outnumbered Finchley by at least 100 youths. And I immediately sensed victory because in a cowardly act the Finchley mob had put their youngest at the front, and small children were between our crew and the Finchley youths, who also carried horrifying weapons like hammers and meat cleavers.

I glanced at Tom at my side, and was grateful to see the bulky form of Errol standing behind him. There was that seemingly eternal moment while the two armies eyed each other, and then someone yelled: 'All together, all together', pronouncing the *th* as *vv*, so it sounded like 'Aw tagevva'. And 200 youths took up the cry as we sprinted forward, Tom and me leading the way.

Suddenly behind us there was a different cry. And no longer was there the thundering of many boots following hard on our heels. The two of us stopped and wheeled. Our men were running the other way! About 100 Finchley youths, perhaps the meanest of their gang, had circled behind using the back streets they knew so well as our crew was led into the trap. Now the trap was sprung, and no longer did we have the edge in numbers, and certainly not in that most vital of tactical elements – surprise.

The fight was vicious. Horrible wounds were inflicted that night as our surrounded mob fought like trapped beasts. Youths were stabbed, children beaten, and blood ran in the streets. The battle raged only for about ten minutes before the police arrived, but it was long enough for Finchley and Archway youths to do their worst to each other. Miraculously, no one was killed, but many still bear scars of that vicious and bloody crew-fight.

There were a number of arrests. The papers the next day were full of news of riots and gang warfare in Finchley involving a mob from Archway. And I was battle-hardened at the tender age of thirteen, even if I was well developed for my age.

5: 'Reggae moon stomp'

I still looked up to my brother, Vernon, who was now in a somewhat superior and better organised crew called 'Summers Town'. They fought in different territory and always carried a certain amount of glamour in my eyes. Eventually I persuaded Vernon to let me run with the Town, and it was then the glamour faded for the brawls that I saw and the gangs that were given a going-over all amounted to a rather sordid affair.

One day I and a few thugs from the Town crew were walking along a street when we saw two Pakistanis, a father and his son.

'Hey, look at these Pakis,' said one of the youths I was with. 'Let's go and give them a kickin'.'

Half-a-dozen skinheads, two of us West Indians, the rest white, inexplicably bore down swooping on the unsuspecting father and son and put the boot in. I was among them, feeling the crunch of bones as my hard toe-cap dug mercilessly into the old man's rib cage.

People just stood and watched the spectacle, except for those who pretended not to see and hurried past. We left the two Pakistanis bruised, humiliated and bleeding in the street. I remembered vividly the look of fear and pain in the teenage boy's face as we left him broken, bleeding and doubled up in pain.

Favourite hunting grounds for trouble were local funfairs. There the various crews would look for each other and fight among the roundabouts and stalls as terrified children looked on.

If money was short, my friends and I would roll people for cash. Literally beat them up and rob them for cash in front of hundreds of people who couldn't care less.

At about this time in my bloodthirsty career I started to

turn more and more to the youth clubs that had sprung up in my area. Putting the boot in was not such good fun without other things in life to give the spice of variety, and there were pretty girls in these clubs.

A disc-jockey kept reggae and pop music alternating on the turntable, with a regular spinning for 'Skinhead Moon Stomp' which was the nearest thing to reggae for skinheads. The aggro was limited here, for dancing and table tennis drained the energy otherwise used for fighting.

In fact, I was glad of the break from bloodshed. In my early teens I had actually seen enough people's skulls shattered with hammers and deep wounds gouged by machetes to turn me gradually away from street fighting. I was tired of seeing people beaten up, and tired of the bruises I got while doling out the aggro.

It was in this tired attitude, at a time when a boy should have been making new and exciting discoveries in life, that I turned to 'Blues'.

Blues were all-night West Indian parties that started at eleven p.m. and went right through to seven a.m. the next day. I would pay my 2/6 at the door of the terraced house at which three or four rooms had been set aside. Loud music flowed non-stop. Cans of beer were on sale, and food. And the atmosphere was hazy and heavy in the packed Blues party. They were jammed solid with West Indians aged from twelve to fifty wearing large floppy tams, berets or woolly hats, adorned in expensive Crombies, smart American brogues, flashy silk handkerchiefs – all the gear that epitomised the black London resurgence of unique identity.

Some wore the new-style dreadlocks – long but thin curls distinct to the new Rastafarian cult which was growing so rapidly in Britain at that time.

At some Blues the records were more frequently of Rastamen, and ganja (marijuana) was passed around more openly. And it all started to get a hold of me, gripping my imagination as a whole new way of socialising unfurled before me. Instead of the bluntly physical communion of violence, here was the challenge of a spiritual fellowship, and with my own kind.

But violence was not unknown at some Blues sessions. Sometimes fights would break out, invariably over petty arguments, and it was not uncommon for someone to be killed.

The culprits were the 'rude' boys. A 'rude' boy or 'rudy' was the West Indian equivalent to the skinhead's hard guy, and because I had been a tough proposition in my earlier setting I now learned how to look after myself in a new environment, mainly by steering clear of 'rudies' when they were upset about something.

I liked Blues. I liked buying my 50 pence worth of ganja, neatly folded in a piece of newspaper, and I liked rolling a 'spliff' for a pleasant evening's smoke. I enjoyed the sensation of being at peace with my surroundings as I floated into new 'highs', and the marked contrast to the heady days of street fighting made it all the more an adventure.

Coupled with this new habit, I began to let my appearance slip. Gone were the smart if unlikely skinhead clothes, and my closely cropped hair was now allowed to grow at random, without the discipline of a regular combing.

I started to take ganja to school where I still mixed with the white boys. There, my close circle of friends and I would smoke pot during breaks, and even on rare occasions took the risk of smoking it in the class when the teacher was otherwise distracted, although only next to an open window to waft away the tell-tale smell. In my usual crafty fashion, I managed to avoid being caught with the illegal drug, although I did on occasions run into deep trouble when I was caught with cigarettes. I didn't realise it, but I was allowing myself to walk headlong into a carefully laid trap that was designed to ensnare my life – anybody's life if they walk into it – and never let go.

The thud, thud, thud of the bass guitar lulled me into a dopey stupor. I looked from black face to black face, and behind the party spirit I saw sadness. These were my brothers, my people. But where did we all come from, and what were our roots? Why had my ancestors been exploited so much and with such cruelty? What right had white men to do such horrible things to my people? And even through the lazy haze of pot smoke, the new friends I had made found it in themselves to be angry, and that anger welled up in me also.

6: African hero

Freedom, O freedom
O freedom over me,
Before I be a slave,
I'll skip over my grave,
And I'll go home
To my father and to be free.

That song caught my imagination. I felt trapped, although I did not fully understand what had happened to me. I wanted peace inside and freedom from the things that nagged remorselessly at my conscience.

My new friends talked of Jah and Ras Tafari, and it sparked something off inside me. Ras Tafari (the ending pronounced 'eye') was Haile Selassie, emperor of Ethiopia and hailed as saviour of black people. Many songs were being sung about him, and more and more he was in my mind, and I felt simultaneously as if I was searching and finding.

I wanted identity. I wanted someone I could relate to, and I wanted spiritual reality. I had been attracted by so much talk about the Rastaman, and this seemed to be the avenue that would lead to the inner Utopia that now gripped my imagination.

I determined to know more about Rastafarians and I eagerly devoured the philosophical answers to my incessant questions. With this new-found way, I stopped my aggressive involvement in the youth scene of those days and embarked on a new, peaceful, approach to life.

Vernon chose to ignore this new direction I was taking, and instead mixed with hippies. And my schoolfriends dropped away one by one as I found new colleagues.

What began as a search took me deeper and deeper as I

turned my thoughts to Africa. I even decided I wanted to go to the dark continent where my ancestral roots were. I looked around and saw the treatment handed out to my black brothers and saw police harassment and ignorant discrimination.

I began to wonder why my parents had brought me to a land where I had to make a go of life, but knew somehow Jah would look after me and help me get over all my problems. And the great mystical being would also somehow help me to get to Africa one day.

I also noticed that my own people were divided. They were frequently malicious towards one another and their priorities seemed all wrong. The black brotherhood needed to sort itself out. Many West Indian girls were having several children before they were even eighteen, and that appalled me. West Indians called themselves brothers and sisters but still the men were abusing their young women and not showing then love and respect, and certainly not caring for them. The men and youths fought with each other, using fearful weapons. They even killed one another.

I spent many evenings in deep discussion with my new friends around an open Bible, talking about the black man, about Africa, and West Indians. We talked about going to Africa. We talked about God and how he created black men. We smoked ganja in a communal pipe that was passed around like the Red Indian's peace pipe. All night long we delved deeper into what we thought was the truth to set us free.

On Sundays, the hazy discussions would start in the early afternoon, centring on Jah (God) and our 'Jesus', Haile Selassie. The Jesus of the Christians was a white man's saviour, but Jah had raised up a new 'Jesus' for black men.

One evening I was at a friend's house to watch a television programme in which my new hero was to make an appearance. Haile Selassie was to talk about the Ethiopian civil war. I was excited and full of eager anticipation.

The great man climbed out of a huge, shining limousine,

casting coins to the impoverished crowds of Addis Ababa. His regal attitude belied his small stature, yet he seemed so far removed from his subjects and was only concerned with a token gesture of compassion.

It was at this moment that my faith in this man began to crumble. On the very first occasion I set my eyes on Haile Selassie, I knew this man was a mere mortal and not 'God', for if he was divine, surely he could do something more for his suffering people? But I was still trapped by something and still I searched in the Rastafarian way for the answers.

Not long after the occasion of the television broadcast, I met Zac, a man with whom I found a strange mutual trust. The tall and thin West Indian spoke freely of Jesus and his miraculous provision for Zac's family, and how it was possible for a man to actually have a meaningful relationship with God.

Zac would stuff endless tracts peddling his brand of Christianity into my pockets. One day, I pulled out one of these small leaflets and read it while I was at my sister's house. It was a small event that prompted a prophetic remark by Lemina, who thought I was merely skipping from one fad to another.

'You goin' to be a preacher man now?' she goaded me.

'No,' I replied, 'but a man has to look into these things because these are the words of the Almighty.'

And the Almighty, who had had his hand on my life ever since it began seventeen years previously, at last found the kind of response he had looked for in me for so long.

7: The search

The words I read in that tract bored deep into my mind and heart. They puzzled me. Somehow I felt as if I was groping for something that I could not fully understand, so I read and re-read the message contained in the pamphlet.

I was being driven by the same force that put me in touch with Bones. Bones was older than me by a few years, yet the two of us had a common desire to understand unseen things. While I began to delve into Rastafarianism, Bones had looked into Roman Catholicism for his answers. As a result he had a very religious approach complete with crucifixes and pictures of saints pinned to the walls of his room. He didn't like me smoking ganja and tried everything he knew to discourage the habit, but without success.

One day, soon after I had been given the tract by Zac, the two of us walked together the 5 miles from a youth club in Kentish Town to the home of my 'woman' in Finsbury Park.

It was a walk that took us into deep, involved and gesticulating conversation.

'Watcha y'know, Bones. We gotta check wiv God for de almighty ways are pass' findin' out, man. We gotta check out what dem are, an' what 'im goin' on wit,' I began.

'Yeah, cos it's not jus' Blues, women an' smokin' spliff dat's all in life,' replied Bones.

'But ah feel say a man mus' check out where 'im goin' to. Because I'm talkin' about people an' talkin' 'bout the judgment of de Almighty, but ah don' know what I'm really reasonin' about. It becomes as folly, man. I tell my woman, "you gotta check for de Almighty an' check about a man call' Jesus". But my woman she say, "what 'bout dis?" An' ah reason wiv 'er dat what ah'm really concerned about is de Almighty. Bible say a man have to work out "is own salvation wiv fear an' tremblin",' I said.

'Yeah, goin' to church is a ting dats important an' I feel say well dat a man mus' go to church an' mus' learn to love de Lord. An' de only way you can do dat, man, is to have de Almighty as God in your life. When ah look around an' see Blues an' see men fightin' wiv each other an' see de youth behavin' bad, ah say, when a man meets de Almighty, it makes 'im diff'rent. He will walk diff'rent. People will know dis is a diff'rent man. Some people might think we are stupid goin' to church, but you cannot worry 'bout dat, y'know. Ah jus' have to serve de Almighty,' continued Bones.

'Seen. [I understand]. Dat's right, man. Because a man had to look at tings an' deal wi' de Almighty an' Him alone,' I answered.

The conversation wound on and on, like a mountain mule track, sometimes going somewhere, and sometimes doubling back, until Bones and I arrived at our destination with some degree of surprise. Our talking had frittered away the time and the long walk had seemed like just a few minutes.

Bones and I were talking about God because Zac had provoked us in his witnessing. But where was Zac? I had to find him and I didn't know where to look. I didn't even know what kind of church he went to, let alone where it was.

The noise is eerie, haunting. It sounds like women wailing. Clearer now. Women singing. The singing is pulling, drawing. What are those words? 'Oh Lord' and 'Jesus took my sin'. What do they mean? It's that building they are pulling me towards. Now the rhythm is clearer. Tambourines. Joy and happiness. Must go in. There they are. All dressed in long blue robes. Wearing funny hats. All the same. There's Zac. I've found him! Why's he beckoning? I must go forward. Go forward. Go to Zac . . .

The alarm shrilled, smashing its noisy way around my brain, wrenching me back into consciousness, clutching at every fibre of my being and stealing cruelly the sleep from my body. I rubbed my eyes. I stared around the dark bedroom, with the reality of the dream steadily fading. I sat up in bed and hoped Zac really was there to answer my hungry questioning, to tell me the way to peace. But he wasn't there, and this was another day. Then I must have dozed off, because I slipped into another dream.

The hot Carribbean sun beat down on the vast expanse of red, blistered neck. The fat evangelist sweated profusely, and rolled the ubiquitous fat cigar around his parched, cracked lips. He wore his grubby khaki sun hat to protect his bald head from the worst of the sun's relentless anger, and his huge ex-army shirt had vast rings of sweat under each arm. He blinked as the salty sweat ran into his eyes.

This time he wasn't preaching. He was sitting in the middle of a huge congregation of children and young people, plus the occasional adult, like a huge white monument in the middle of a black sea. The preacher was a West Indian. He was very young, in his teens. He was strongly built and certainly not lost for words as he spoke with fire to his own people.

'God loves you. Jesus loves you.' The words tripped off his tongue with powerful relevance. 'He cares for you. For God so loved the world that he gave himself for you and for me. Look around and see the blessings of God. And God has a big, bright mansion in glory for you. Give him your heart. Give him your life. And he will give you his Father's kingdom . . .' Then suddenly I realised, with a force that woke me up, that the preacher was me.

The dream was so vivid, even after I had fully woken up. I wondered why I should dream such a strange thing, and remember so clearly the fat American missionary. 'Les, what are you doin,' I thought to myself, 'you're not a preacher-man.' I was puzzled, and intrigued.

Then I met a girl called Lilly at a fun-fair in West Hampstead and found my searching for God was even affecting my relationships with women. When I chatted her up it turned out she was the sister of a black youth called Davison who had clearly 'got religion'.

Davison had got himself quite a reputation by shouting

out 'Hallelujah' at the top of his voice in various public places, and was generally thought to be crazy. But if his behaviour was the result of a genuine spiritual experience, I wanted to find out about it.

I asked Lilly about her brother's conversion. 'Oh, he jus' came home one day an' announced he was followin' dis Jesus,' she said.

So I asked her if she had any experience of God. She hadn't, although she said she thought she believed in him. And all of a sudden I lost interest in this pretty little girl, because I wanted to find a greater reality, and she seemed unable to shed any light on the pathway along which I was groping.

Bones agreed with the diagnosis that this youth Davison must be crazy, if only because he shouted out religious slogans that embarrassed everyone. 'You wanna keep clear of dis man,' was his advice.

But on the occasions when I later saw Davison, I realised that this was a man who had peace and joy, even if he did act a bit strange from time to time.

But now God was more important to me than people, and certainly more important than casual relationships. Even as a teenager, I had found the Rastafarian ideal of having a number of women to sleep with and call my own a satisfying way of life. But now I was searching for God. And God was more important than women. It was like sitting at a table spread with a sumptious feast and losing your appetite.

8: Mother

After leaving school in 1973 at the age of sixteen I became an apprentice plumber. During my seventeenth year, when I was at the height of my search for God, I used my mother's home as a base and gave her a cut of my £11 take-home pay. My parents had been divorced for some years, and my mother looked after me and the others well. Often I would disappear for days, sleeping at the home of one of my 'women', and return unannounced. My mother didn't worry about that.

But in 1974 she was taken ill. When I returned from a five-day absence, Vernon told me that she had got worse and the doctor had been. She looked drawn and frail, appearing much older than her thirty-eight years, and I took her immediately to hospital.

She lay in the hospital bed in the clinical atmosphere and was barely conscious. She seemed in a daze. I sat for hours with her, and once, near the end, she caught my eye with renewed awareness and her look said: 'How will they cope without me?' I felt cold, and suddenly alone.

That night I found Vernon in a West End club and told him how she was. We both knew she was dying, but didn't understand why or from what. The next day the whole family visited the hospital, and this time we were ordered to wear white gowns and breathing masks before we could see the withering, barely breathing wisp of a human being that was our mother. She looked far worse, and there was an atmosphere of gloom and death in the ward. She had appeared to have deteriorated to the point of death overnight.

Her eyes opened. In a slow, croaking voice, she asked for water. I immediately remembered the saying that I had learnt in Antigua that when someone who was dying asked for water they were about to go. I braced myself. But she held on.

I spent the evening at the Bluesville club in Wood Green and went on to the home of the girl I was with at that time. The next morning I was up in good time for a college plumbing course I was attending, and as I went out through the front door, and kissed the girl goodbye, something strange happened. I was sure I heard a voice. It wasn't the girl, and there was no one else nearby. But I had the clear impression of a voice saying: 'You will be told this morning that your mother has died.' I was shaken.

Half-way through a page of theory notes the lecture room door opened and a member of staff at the college poked his head around the door. 'Is there a Les Isaac here?' he asked.

My heart started to beat rapidly. My legs went weak. And this seemingly tough black guy could hardly speak. I had to cough and splutter before I could identify myself, by which time all the other members of the class had turned round and were staring at me with cold, disinterested eyes. I knew by the look on the man's face what he was going to say.

'Your mother has just died,' he confirmed.

Zombie-like, I left the room in a daze. I didn't know what I was doing or where I was going, I just walked like an automaton. And when I found the rest of my family, they were in the same state.

Three days later I saw my mother's body in the coffin, and for the first time in my life the full reality of death dawned on me. As a youth I had several times handled a weapon not caring if it took another's life, but I did not know what death was really like. I was deeply moved, and it was as if a sharp knife had been suddenly plunged into my soul, for now I saw without fully understanding. I had seen people die by pretence in the cinema, and had equated the death of people on newsreels as the same fake thing. Now I saw the reality of death, and it had taken my mother.

From that moment, I found myself pleading with the mystical figure of Selassie to intervene. I started to smoke more ganja than could possibly be good for me, and my conversation was continually of Rastafarianism. Morning and evening, I dowsed my feelings in marijuana and Ras Tafari.

By the time my mother was buried, my father had returned home. A short, stocky and strong West Indian, his arrival brought new tensions to the Isaac household, and particularly between me and him.

He was a man of authority, not used to anyone questioning him. What he said went—and that was an explosive thing for me to encounter. It was as if my father intended to carry on in the same way as he had when he last saw me as a youngster who needed a good dressing-down from time to time. The new arrival in his forties, wearing his donkey jacket, jeans and cloth cap, was a threat, and he frequently squared up to Vernon and me.

The main bone of contention was the way I would stay away from home without announcing my plans and then a few days later turn up on the doorstep.

'Where you sleep, boy?' asked my father in his gruff voice.

'Watcha, ole man. Awha' ya goin' on with?' (What are you saying?)

'Listen me, boy. No more dem sleepin' out.'

'Watcha, Dad, you no talkin' to a boy. You are dealin' with a *man*.'

I spoke the word *man* with a deep breath and drawn out for emphasis. And as I spoke the word, my eyes flashed to back up my claim to manhood.

In response, it brought a threat from my father: 'If you think you more man than me, sleep out again an' see what happens.'

Something snapped inside me. I stepped past my father, went to my room and packed a few things into a small bag. I left the house. When I returned a few days later with the threat still in my mind I was ready to actually fight with my father. It didn't come to that, because the threat had been an empty one. But it didn't herald an end to the violent arguments that raged between us.

One day I came home to find my sister in tears. My father had taken it upon himself to mete out some kind of physical punishment all round, and it brought a renewed conflict between us. Protectively, I demanded to know what my father was doing.

'Dats no business of yours,' was the reply.

It wasn't long before the potentially explosive incident had developed to the point where we squared up to each other again, fists clenched and ready to fight.

'Dad, listen . . . I was a rude boy at school. An' I used to fight and do these things. But now I'm a Rasta and I don' deal with violence.' I hoped my father wouldn't fight, not so much because of my philosophy of peace, but more because I knew I could hurt him.

The two of us stared at each other with red eyes for several minutes. Then I dropped my fists and walked away.

The conflict continued day in day out, until finally the question was put: how can there be more than one captain on a ship?

Vernon, as the older brother the heir to authority in the home, calmly told my father he should leave. But he didn't go, and the friction got worse.

I was eventually provoked into hunting for the old machete my mother had sensibly thrown out. My new ethics discarded, I searched high and low for the weapon that would surely bring my father to submission. I couldn't find it, and made up my mind to get a new one from the army surplus store the next day. Fortunately, I couldn't get away from work during my lunchbreak the next day, for my anger had not subsided and I would have gladly bought the lethal weapon which, with my strength behind it, could have killed my father in a single blow.

That evening as I headed for the store, I passed a restaurant where my cousin George worked as a chef. I wanted to see how he was and, as it was only minutes until George finished work, I went into the open mission hall next door to wait. There, sitting in a corner sipping a cup of tea, was a skinny Nigerian. And it turned out this Nigerian was looking for someone to talk to, because talking was his favourite pastime.

Amos the preacher was the type of Christian who does not believe in luck or chance. So when I stepped inside, a strong and angry looking youth, Amos was going to preach. And the way he put the story of Jesus made it almost appear on a screen before my eyes. I could see Calvary, I could see the soldiers, I could hear the thud of hammer on nail and the cry of agony as the huge wooden cross thudded home into its slot and Jesus was left to die.

I never went to the army surplus stores. I didn't buy a new machete, and I didn't slice open my father's skull. Instead I talked with God.

It was God who spoke first. For the vivid description Amos had given me had created an atmosphere in which I just seemed to be able to commune with the One for whom I had been searching so long.

'Les, Rasta is not the way,' the voice in my mind said.

'Selassie is not the way. I am the way. And I am the truth, and the life as well. Les, depart from your sin.'

During the half-hour walk home, I knew I had been talking to Someone as clearly as the conversation I had held with Bones. And during that walk, I decided I wanted to become a Christian. I wanted to know God. At that moment an awe-inspiring fear came upon me, a fear of judgment, a fear that if I were to die or this Jesus were to come back there and then, I would have no excuses and I would be lost. And what could I say to the Son of God? I then had one of those experiences, normally reserved for people facing death, when I saw in an instant my whole life spread before me and it didn't look very good.

When I arrived home, without a machete and in a totally different mood, I announced to my family that I was going to become a Christian. They all ignored me because they were watching television.

'I said I am goin' to become a Christian,' I repeated.

'Oh yea?' said Lemina without any interest whatsoever. 'You always comin' up with funny ideas. Leave us alone cos we are watchin' dis programme.'

I went to my room, and there I stayed all night, although I was unable to sleep for thinking about God. I thought about the death of Jesus as described by Amos, the man from the mission, and I thought about the possible return of Christ when I wasn't ready for it. I decided that after work the next day I would go straight to Amos and talk some more with him.

When I got to work, the first person I saw was Chicago, a good friend of mine.

'I'm goin' to become a Christian,' I told him, expecting some kind of slap on the back.

'It's not an easy thing to be a Christian,' was the discouraging reply.

'But if this man Jesus is able to save me, he should be able to keep me too.'

But I couldn't find Amos that day after work, and I couldn't find the final piece of the jigsaw that I knew would give me peace of mind. I couldn't sleep for several nights. I became bleary-eyed and sluggish at work. I felt as though my life was full of poison that needed to be removed, but I didn't know how to go about it and I didn't know how to pray. Many times I fell down beside my bed and tried to pray, but I only felt dumb. I felt I had been dumb all my life, and now when I needed words to speak they just wouldn't come. Instead tears came to my eyes. I felt guilty and so dirty before the Almighty God whose presence I could now feel in the room. The stronger the presence of God became, the fouler and dirtier I felt. All my sin was before me, and I knew it to be offensive to this holy Being.

I again struggled to speak. I thought the Lord's prayer might be appropriate, for people in films always seemed to say the Lord's prayer when they needed help. I opened my mouth again and forced myself to speak.

But I could only say, with deep sobs, 'Jesus, you know I don't believe in you, but if you are real, I want you to save me.'

After what seemed an age, I got off my knees, and stood in front of my full-length wardrobe mirror.

'Wotcha, a big man like you cryin'?' I said to the reflection. I stood staring at the mirror for some time, and then felt as if I was looking through the mirror at something in the wardrobe. My eyes were piercing the glass and the wood and I was looking at a small package in the pocket of one of my jackets. It was ganja. I opened the wardrobe and pulled out the weed which was wrapped in a small piece of newspaper. I opened the window and threw it out with the words, 'I don't need you no more.'

Immediately a voice said, 'Les, you crazy or somethin'?' But I renewed my vow. 'I don't need this no more.'

I looked in the mirror again. I saw my rasta locks, long, and thick; they had not seen a comb for years.

'You don't need your locks to be a child of God,' I told myself. 'Now you need to let people know you are a child of God, and you don't need locks for that.'

Within a few days, I had my hair cut, and my own glory was removed to make way for the inner glory that God had brought, and at last my family took notice of me. My friends at the clubs took note of me as well, for they thought me a little mad or at least off colour to refuse their offers of ganja. And my talk of going to church was surely just a passing phase, wasn't it? That's what they thought.

9: New life

I hunted for Amos and brought tears of joy to the little Nigerian's face when I told him what had happened. We spent many hours together, an older, experienced Christian encouraging a spiritually new-born West Indian and showing me the ways of God.

'You're a different person now,' Amos told me. 'The world will look different, and people will seem different to you. They might even turn against you, strange as it seems, 'cos you'll be a threat to them now. Some people jus' get all hot and bothered 'cos they think you're preaching at them just because you say you prayed this morning or if you mention God.'

I decided it couldn't be true of my friends.

'But you mus' realise you've got new friends now,' Amos went on. 'First you've got Jesus. No friend better than Jesus. He's always there, always listening, always with you. Then you got friends like me. An' I think we'll find you some more friends, Les.

'You keep prayin'. There ain't no substitute for talkin' with the Lord. It's the source of your strength, talkin' to the Lord. Read the Scriptures, and talk to God about them. Ask him to explain them to you. Let the Holy Spirit dwell in you and live in you to show you the way to live. Let him speak through you, 'cos he saved you to make you into a window so that people can see heaven when they see you.'

Amos told me to meet him by the Vauxhall underground the following Sunday at a quarter to eleven. He was travelling to Watford to preach at a church there, but on his return he said he would take me to a church that would make me feel at home and where I could make some new friends.

The Thomases were old friends of our family. They lived

in a council flat in Camden, and always appreciated a visit from me or my brothers and sisters. But Mrs Thomas and her five daughters got quite a shock the following Thursday night when I walked through the door.

'Where your locks?' they demanded in unison. The girls giggled.

The sight of me with short hair and no tam hat was quite a shock to the system.

'I've become a Christian,' I announced. The Thomas family didn't know whether to laugh or take it seriously. They were just numbed with shock, not fully understanding what I meant.

'I gave my life to Jesus,' I said, 'and between us we decided these locks mus' go. I also threw my ganja away, 'cos I'm a new person.'

The Thomas family was still in a state of shock.

'My life was a mess, Mrs Thomas, an' I needed to let God take over an' help me get straight,' I continued. 'I done so many bad things, an' I felt so sinful, I just knew God wanted me to let him change me. So I searched and searched, I asked people, an' eventually I found out that all you have to do is ask God's forgiveness, receive his love, an' let him come right in. It's called bein' *born again*.'

I had found the right expression, and spoke it with that customary deep breath and wide eyes, drawing out the words for maximum effect. The Thomases stared at me.

'An' I can assure you I'm a new person, completely diff'rent. I feel diff'rent. I knows I'm diff'rent. An' I want people to know they can be Christians, too. 'Fact, I can't understand why people keep on livin' the way they do when they can have all the peace an' joy they ever wanted by jus' turning to Jesus. Ah mean, Mrs Thomas, I tought Rastafari was the one. I thought Selassie would help me. But he didn't. I begged him to help, but there was nothin' there. Jus' emptiness. But now I got peace and joy and I feel diff'rent.'

I was coming to a crescendo, and still the Thomases had their eyes riveted on me.

'Why, you can do the same too. You can give your lives to Jesus. I'm tellin' you, this is the only way . . .'

At this point Mrs Thomas found the reserve to speak up. I felt like Samson, with an inner strength welling up, and Mrs Thomas was beginning to feel like one of the strongman's victims.

'Yes, well, Les dear, this is very nice for you,' she said with a smile, emphasising the 'you' as if to say, 'keep it to yourself'. 'It's good you've made a change an' you are doin' this, boy, it's the best way. I do wish your mother was here to see the way you've changed.'

I didn't take any hint that the subject should be changed: I didn't even realised Mrs Thomas was not about to fall to her knees to beg for forgiveness. Indeed I thought she would. So I went on with my story and spoke with firm confidence about my new life.

When I left the flat I felt a warm glow deep inside, and I realised for the first time that a greater Being had been speaking through me. True, my words may have had a measure of immaturity and a lack of tact about them, but it had been God who had stirred me and God who had used me to put the most important message of life across. I had been God's mouthpiece.

The joy of speaking for the One who now meant so much to me gripped my imagination. I felt as if I wanted to tell everyone, and a new drive was now evident in my life. I realised that through my teens my motivation had been running out of steam – my earlier ride on life's roundabout of excitement had tailed off into dissatisfaction with a religious movement that had nothing tangible to offer except getting high on drugs. Now I knew I had reality, and that reality was deeply satisfying.

When I awoke the next morning after speaking to the Thomas family, I drew back my bedroom curtains to look out on a new world. I still saw the dingy Camden streets, litter lying in the road, and rusting cars parked bumper to bumper on each side. But for the first time I saw it as God's world. I was looking out on God's creation, and I saw the potential and the good instead of the depression and deprivation, And I saw how it was man's sin that had given him this lot in life, not bad luck or a mean God, but man's own rebellion. Now I knew what it was like to be free from that sin, and I felt strangely free from the world's clutches.

But at work that day I found out what direct opposition to God was like. I told my workmates that Jesus loved them, but they didn't want to know. They were shocked and threatened by what I told them, and they covered it up by laughing at me. I was indignant. I reverted to the only way I knew and got aggressive, matching their ridicule with threats, as if using my natural strength would somehow get them to see the truth that Jesus changes lives.

That night I went home discouraged. What had I expected? Only that all my friends at work would be falling over themselves to be converted, instantly realising that I was right and everyone needed a saviour and should turn to Jesus. But it just didn't happen like that, and my dream was shattered. I walked home and once again saw the dingy street where I lived and the sense of being trapped in the gloominess of the area got to me.

I went to my room and fell on my knees. I prayed. Lord, why do they not want you? Why do they laugh? Why do they not listen? Gently and with deep love for this fragile child of his, God showed me how his own Son had been horribly and cruelly rejected. How Jesus had brought people healing and life yet had been spat upon, scorned, flayed alive with horrible instruments of death, betrayed and crucified naked for all the world to see. The Christian life was not a series of happy events with everything clicking marvellously into place. It was a war. A struggle between spiritual powers, not between religious ideals and the tradition of men. A fight to the death between the forces of darkness headed by their dark lord Satan and the forces of truth and light, headed by God's own Son, Jesus. And the ultimate triumph and victory had been won there at that point of humiliation, agony and death, at Calvary. The great triumph was won as people wept before the emaciated dying figure of a man who had been frighteningly tortured, because that man was taking on himself the sin and sickness of the world so that everyone might be forgiven and set free.

God's victory was the height of rejection. And I was feeling sorry for myself because my friends had rejected me. Now I saw that here was the place and time to love those who laugh, to pray earnestly for those who scoff. For Jesus, who was enemy of no one but hated by many enemies, said my new way was to love my enemies.

The one exception at work was Chicago. I didn't get any ridicule from the one who had warned me of the difficulties in being a Christian, and I soon found out the reason. Chicago had once committed his life to God, but in the problems of life he encountered had gone back on his word. He had backslidden.

Now Chicago was watching me. He even went to church with me, and he knew the pressures I was going through. He wanted to see how a fiery teenager like me would get on, whether I would make progress or just let my new light fade. Sometimes Chicago and I would sing choruses together at work, and he taught me many new songs of praise to God. That tended to infuriate our workmates even more.

I frequently met old friends in the West End. They all wanted to know where I had been and why hadn't I been to my old haunts? I told them all, with my usual enthusiasm, about the change in my life now that I was a Christian. I wanted them to know this good news and how it would give them something to live for.

One day, soon after my conversion, I was in Leicester Square when I came across a group of young people giving out leaflets and talking to people about Jesus. I immediately decided to go and offer my assistance. But the first member of the group I talked to, a girl, seemed to be suspicious of me. They told me they were from a church in Swiss Cottage, near where I lived, but I felt warned off when they said that many of their youth meetings were discos to keep young people active and interested.

At this point and without realising it, I formed my policy of separation from the things I used to be involved in.

'That's what I used to do all the time,' I told them. 'I've told all my friends I've changed and I've got better things to do. If they all saw me doing the same old things they would think I wasn't serious. You'd better count me out.'

We talked for a little longer before I left them. I was grateful for the experience because it helped me to be certain in my mind what my new boundaries were—boundaries that I was setting for myself—so that I could look back and see the point at which I had left an old life behind and started a new one.

My decision was confirmed to be the right one for me when I had to keep a promise that weekend. Just before my conversion, I had promised to take a girlfriend and her mother out for the evening for a wild rave-up at a club. I decided to keep my word that Saturday night, and the following day I would skip my customary all-day lie-in and go to church.

I took them to a club in Carnaby Street that was a cut above most of the places I went to, and the moment the three of us went in it was like entering a different world. I ate a meal with them, watched a horde of gyrating bodies on the dance floor, danced with my girl no more than three times in the entire evening, and the whole time felt a growing feeling of care and concern for all these people who needed to know that good news which had radically changed my life.

'You wanna smoke a spliff?' The gruff voice jerked me back to a state of alertness. It was an old friend who had spotted me—even without my dreadlocks. 'Take some weed, man?' my friend asked.

'No, man, not for me.' My friend and the two women looked at me strangely as if I was rejecting money. Could this be the same Les? What had happened to the fun-loving Rastaman they knew, who was acting like a fish out of water?

And all I could think was that tomorrow I was going to church to worship God and listen to the Bible taught and that was what I wanted more than anything else in the whole world. Church, the very thing that all my life had been the epitome of boredom, was now the thing I wanted most. I wanted life.

The night dragged on. The girl I was with thought it was the dullest night she had ever experienced. Then eventually, at about four-thirty on that Sunday morning, it was time to go home. I hailed a cab for the girl and her mother, and made my own way home. I sank into bed at five-thirty with the thought on my mind, today I'm going to church!

At eight-thirty I was up and ready. I met Chicago and his wife and a friend of theirs, and the four of us headed for the rendezvous with Amos at Vauxhall. We were there in good time, but eleven o' clock came and there was still no sign of Amos. Eleven-fifteen. We walked around, passed a church out of which came some happy-sounding singing, and wondered if that was the one. Eleven-thirty and no Amos.

'Let's go home,' said Chicago. 'It's no use waitin'.'

'No,' I said with a little more volume than I had intended. 'I know this man and he said he would be here and he will be. Let's wait a bit longer.'

Each train that pulled in at the station made me look for the frail figure of Amos, but he didn't come. My hopes sank, and there were long silences while the four of us just stared at the ground.

Eventually at twelve-fifteen Amos arrived, dashing up the escalator two or three steps at a time, apologising profusely when he saw us waiting. He told us he had been unavoidably delayed and, taking my arm, herded us out of the station foyer and down the street to the very church where we had heard the singing.

'At last,' I thought. 'After all that waiting last night and this morning, I'm going to church. This is where I want to be.'

The building was packed with people. The congregation was mixed, with whites and blacks worshipping happily together, and there was also a fair sprinkling of European immigrants.

It was a large building, and most of the rows of chairs were filled, with just enough spare seats three rows from the front for five latecomers. As we made our way down the aisle, I noticed that the warm, carpeted building also had a spiritual warmth to it. I was happy already.

I sat down. I looked around at the people worshipping. They had just received communion and there was an atmosphere of gratitude among them. They were just finishing a song that I didn't recognise, and then people just shouted and spoke words out loud, like 'Hallelujah' and

'Praise the Lord'. I was amazed.

Then I looked at the minister at the front who was standing with both hands stretched in the air saying 'Hallelujah, hallelujah' over and over again. I found myself wanting to laugh uncontrollably. I found it so amusing – I had never seen anything like this before, and it was hilarious.

But these people had joy. They all had a relationship with Jesus that meant something, just like I had.

The following week, Amos took me to a Methodist church in Holborn where he was based while visiting England to take a Bible College course. The singing was much more subdued in this church, and the people only did what they were told to do according to their tradition. But when the minister went into the pulpit to speak he poured out living words that seemed to me as if they were meant for me alone. It was so uplifting and encouraging, I felt as though I had been washed clean on the inside.

Amos was soon to leave London, and he told me to go back to the church at Vauxhall to get basic teaching about how to live as a Christian and to be baptised. I had heard of the Christian baptism ceremony, and was eager to be immersed. I felt like the Ethiopian eunuch in the story in the book of Acts, and wanted no more delay.

10: A dream?

I may have split my sides laughing when I saw people with their arms in the air shouting to an invisible God, but when I went back to the church at Kennington it wasn't for amusement.

God was becoming more real to me every day, and I knew that to be with other people who had a rich experience of God was important. The church was an apostolic pentecostal church, which meant there was an emphasis on the supernatural. These people believed in miracles. They believed in God speaking through men and women. They believed in healing. And they believed in two kinds of baptism.

The only kind of baptism I had known anything about was the custom of the land in which I lived to sprinkle babies' heads and give them their names in a religious ceremony. It didn't mean anything to me, in fact I didn't know if I had been sprinkled as a baby, but many of my friends had been and their families believed in it wholeheartedly. Yet as I read my Bible I found no reference to baby baptism, but instead I found adults being baptised, and surely not at a fancy stone font? Furthermore, I found references to another baptism – the baptism in the Holy Spirit.

There was no doubt that the emphasis on miracles I now encountered each time I returned to the apostolic church was a genuine thing, and not the figment of anyone's imagination. These people had a power, a driving force, that was not to be found in most people. It was an energy that enabled them to live successful lives in a miserable world. They enjoyed living, while people all around moaned and whined about paltry things like the weather and taxes. They could get up on a Sunday morning and drive to church and instead of making a leisurely entry into the day, they could sing and praise God with great gusto and enthusiasm. They could clap and dance just because God was with them. They could pray for great things, even impossible things, as if the strangest result would be that the thing they asked for didn't happen. They *knew* God, and there was a key to their secret.

It was a cold, frosty February morning when I made my way to the apostolic church, but the atmosphere inside was warm and welcoming. I arrived just as the first hymn was ending: 'Floods of joy o'er my soul, like the sea billows roll, since Jesus came into my heart'. They held out the last note on the word 'heart' as if wanting to savour the truth of the statement they had just sung, and then as it ended there was an eruption of joyful praises with 'hallelujah' and 'I love you Lord' shouted freely from excited hearts. My heart beat faster, and I joined in, feeling the adrenalin begin to flow as if I was running out on to a soccer pitch.

Following prayers said by the minister, which reached a crescendo of praise after about five minutes, people began to rise spontaneously to their feet and testify about their faith in Christ.

'Jesus changed my family,' said one large black lady. 'My, dey needed changin', cos they was in sin,' she went on. 'But Jesus, he came an' made us all new, an' now we is a happy family.'

Her face glowed and a broad smile showed her feelings about this remarkable event, and indeed, sitting either side of her were a pleased-looking husband and three small children.

A teenager stood up next. He was a thin African, wearing faded blue jeans, and his curly black hair was clearly being allowed to grow at random. 'I just want to say . . .' his voice was nervous, 'that I didn't ever think I would be able to pass my exams . . .' he coughed in embarrassment, 'but I prayed to God to help me do my best, and I felt so calm when the day came, and I just want to say that yesterday I heard that I had passed them all. I'm so grateful to Jesus.' He sat down, and a murmur of appreciation went around the large auditorium. Many hadn't been able to hear him, because he was so quietly spoken, but they still smiled with the youth, recognising that God was working in him for good.

Next, an elderly woman took her chance to speak of her moment of triumph. 'I prayed for years for my son to become a Christian,' she said in a loud, clear voice, which didn't seem to go with her frail frame. 'I prayed every day for him, even when he shouted at me and said horrible things about God. When he started gambling, I prayed even more, and when he lost everything I knew it could be the time when he would turn to God.

'Well, last week I had a letter from him . . .' her voice suddenly quivered with emotion, and she stopped for a moment. The church was silent. 'He gave his life to Jesus and he is now part of a pentecostal church in America.' The 200 or so people suddenly burst into a round of praise.

With a word from the minister, the congregation started praying and the same message of gratitude came across as people rose to their feet to talk with God, each with a different way of communicating, and all so grateful to a loving, caring Father. Then came more singing, and midway through a hymn of worship I thought to myself 'Hey, man, is this really you? Are you really in church? You mus' be dreamin'.'

The memory of that vivid dream when I had been preaching the gospel in Antigua came flooding back, and for a moment I wondered if this too was just a dream. But it wasn't. It was real. So very, very real.

Normally at twelve noon on a Sunday morning I would be fast asleep in bed after an all-night Blues, but here I was in church, and joining in, too! Before this, I had just thought of church as rows of dowdy people doing boring things, but now church to me was life itself, and to miss it was unthinkable. This was food and drink to me now. And I knew it was because the One these people were singing and talking about was real, and he was there, present in that very building and communing with his people. It was real, but at the same time almost unreal. Different. Like nothing I had ever experienced before. Here there was no doubt that this Jesus was Lord, and the most powerful Being in the whole of creation. Yet this great, awesome, Being was here in a building, and what was even more amazing, he had time for me. A black seventeen-year-old, guilty of many secret and open crimes, a social outcast, was at peace with God and actually talking and listening to his Son Jesus Christ. Remarkable. The sheer impact of it made me sit down in my seat while everyone else carried on singing . . .

> This is my story, this is my song,
> Praising my Saviour all the day long . . .

It seemed to be the favourite hymn, but it summed up the most remarkable few days in my life. I had a new story, and a new song. It was about my Saviour, a man called Jesus who was also the Son of God.

11: Baptism

But as for Philip, an angel of the Lord said to him, 'Go over to the road that runs from Jerusalem through the Gaza Desert, arriving around noon.' So he did, and who should be coming down the road but the Treasurer of Ethiopia, a eunuch of great authority under Candace the queen. He had gone to Jerusalem to Worship at the Temple, and was now returning in his chariot, reading aloud from the book of the prophet Isaiah.

The Holy Spirit said to Philip, 'Go over and walk along beside the chariot!'

Philip ran over and heard what he was reading and asked, 'Do you understand it?'

'Of course not!' the man replied. 'How can I when there is no one to instruct me?' And he begged Philip to come up into the chariot and sit with him.

The passage of Scripture he had been reading from was this:

'He was led as a sheep to the slaughter, and as a lamb is silent before the shearers, so he opened not his mouth;

'In his humiliation, justice was denied him; and who can express the wickedness of the people of his generation? For his life is taken from the earth.'

The eunuch asked Philip, 'Was Isaiah talking about himself or someone else?'

So Philip began with this same Scripture and then used many others to tell him about Jesus.

As they rode along, they came to a small pool of water, and the eunuch said, 'Look – water! Why can't I be baptized?'

'You can,' Philip answered, 'if you believe with all your heart.'

And the eunuch replied, 'I believe that Jesus Christ is the Son of God.'

He stopped the chariot, and they went down into the water and Philip baptized him. And when they came up out of the water, the Spirit of the Lord caught away Philip, and the eunuch never saw him again, but went on his way rejoicing. (Acts 8.26–40).

As the service drew to a close, I slowly became more aware of the world around me, of hunger, of the fact that I had to catch an underground train to get home, and I became more aware of the people in the meeting. I looked at my watch. The service had been going on for two hours, but whereas that sort of time for a church meeting would have been unthinkable to me before, now it seemed far too short. It seemed that at the moment of climax, the meeting was ending when it should be going on, and I felt that I could go on into the afternoon. This was real life to me now.

After about three weeks as a new Christian, I was beginning to come up with some answers to my inner qeustioning about baptism. I still didn't know what baptism in the Holy Spirit was, but I was now aware that every convert should be baptised in water by full immersion.

One Sunday evening the assistant pastor at the church, David Perry, was preaching about the love Jesus has for his children. It was a simple, direct challenge to people to respond to the love that Christ had demonstrated by going to the cross at Calvary to die in the place of everyone who had sinned. He explained that meant literally everyone who had ever lived, for the only person who had lived a sinless life was Jesus himself, yet he had died to take on himself the punishment for everyone else's sin.

As he finished, the preacher said: 'I want everyone to bow their heads in prayer.' Everyone did. 'If you really want to become a Christian, or if you want to give everything to him, I want to pray for you. If the Lord has been challenging you over something in your life, then now is the moment to get it sorted out. I want you to rise to your feet right now.'

There was silence for several seconds and nobody moved.

I felt a deep, inner conviction, and I wasn't sure why. I felt moved to stand up, but I was scared and nervous.

Just then the preacher said, 'If you are feeling nervous about what I am asking you to do, then instead of standing, just put your hand up so that I can pray for you.' It was as if he knew exactly what was going through my mind.

I immediately put my hand up, and the pressure lifted. I no longer felt frightened, and instead I felt good inside. Other people were putting their hands up, and each time the pastor uttered a heartfelt 'God bless you' to them. 'As soon as the service is over,' he said, 'I want to see all of you who stood or who put your hands up in the counselling room.'

The preacher spoke to us for about ten minutes about baptism, the very thing that had been on my mind. He said there was to be a baptism service in three weeks' time, and which of us who had responded that night were going to do what the Scriptures said? I was the first to say 'I want to be baptised', and my eagerness brought a smile to the pastor's face. Everyone who had gone into the counselling room agreed to be baptised.

Three weeks later, the Sunday night baptism service came. I sat in the front row with eight others, each of us with a nervous expectation showing in our faces. I wondered just how it would all work out, as I looked at the clear blue water in the baptismal tank that was built into the church's raised platform.

The nine of us had been told that it would be appreciated if we would say a few words before being baptised, speaking about the reasons why we were doing this, and what God had come to mean to us.

David Perry and the minister, Pastor Kane, came in and the service began. As the time approached for baptising, I looked nervously around and saw a packed church. I tried to formulate a message in my mind that I would give when my turn came. I would speak about how I became a Christian, and how God had been so good to me, and how I had already seen the miraculous intervention of the Lord in my life in little ways.

I was still trying to memorise a speech when my name

was called. I was the fourth to be baptised. I turned to the congregation, looked at them nervously as I realised not one word of my carefully prepared speech had stayed in my mind, and opened my mouth to speak.

'Er . . . thank God for saving me,' I said, a little shocked at the clarity of my own voice, and at the same time wondering if everyone was quiet because they were interested in that remarkable statement. 'Please pray for me.' That was all I said, but it came from the heart, and there were many loud 'Amens' and 'Praise God' phrases shouted out. I felt good, and turned towards the water tank where Pastor Kane stood up to his waist in water.

I stepped into the tank, feeling my jeans cling as they got wet. I took the pastor's hand as the two of us stood there. I thought how warm the water felt, and I was glad I wasn't shivering.

'Les Isaac,' the pastor said in a loud, booming voice, 'on the confession of your faith, I now baptise you in the name of the Father, the Son and the Holy Spirit.' With that there was a great splash as I went backwards into the water and under.

The blue water closed over my head with a rush, and it swirled around my body, encasing me, entombing me momentarily in my watery grave. The whole event took a split second, but in that moment there came a revelation to me that I was being buried with Christ. I went under. I was put under. Just like Jesus when he was put in the tomb. This was the symbolic end to my old life, the old Les was dead, and just as surely as Jesus rose from the dead, I would come up from that water and be aware of my new life of total dedication to God.

I surfaced. I flicked my head and sent drips flying all over the platform and over the people nearest to the tank. I rubbed the water from my eyes.

I threw my arms into the air and uttered thanks to God, in just the same way that had made me laugh the first time I came to the church. It was a beautiful experience, and the outward symbolism had touched me deep in my life in a moment I would never forget.

I felt ready to talk to anyone about my Lord. In fact, the experience of baptism gave me a renewed impetus in my explosive desire to share my exciting discovery with people, although now the feelings of aggression when someone was not prepared to accept my belief were going. I no longer wanted to beat the truth into people.

During one of my customary sessions reading the Bible, I found the words in Zechariah that said: 'Not by might, nor by power, but by my Spirit, saith the Lord', and I at last understood how a person comes to see and understand God for himself. Who had picked me up by the lapels to make me into a Christian? No one. God had gently and patiently revealed Christ to me by the working of his own Holy Spirit in the circumstances of life. So now I realised that forcing God on people would do no good at all, and in fact could only do harm. The revelation made me feel rather stupid, and I dropped to my knees to pray.

'Help me to speak to people,' I pleaded. 'Help me to speak your words, and to speak to them the way you want me to speak to them. Help me to really love people.'

And while I prayed, I had a growing feeling of certainty that as I talked to people about Jesus, God would save them. I just knew that this was how it would be.

Three months after my conversion, I went back to some of my old youth club haunts to see old friends. They hadn't seen me in that time and had no idea I had become a Christian, and I wondered how my new attitude in life would go down with them.

I walked along Hampstead Road towards one club where I knew many of my friends would be, and I spotted a girl I hadn't seen for some time, waiting at a bus stop.

'Hello,' I said cockily.

She looked at me strangely, her head tilted to one side. She stared at me for what seemed like several minutes, and then recognition dawned on her face.

'I can't believe it,' she exclaimed. 'Where's your locks?'

'I'm a Christian now,' I replied. 'I don't need no locks any more.'

We talked excitedly together for ten minutes about old times, about who was going out with whom, and I managed to explain a little of what had happened to me. Then the girl's bus came and she left, stunned by the difference in me.

What are my friends going to say now that the news is out that I'm a Christian? I thought. Will they laugh at me? Or will they accept me with my new faith, as they did when I became a Rastafarian?

Just then I heard a loud voice shout out, 'Rasta, was 'appened?'

I wheeled round to see a West Indian boy who had run in the same gang as me, but who now had dreadlocks every bit as long as mine had been.

'I've become a Christian, man,' I said.

Within seconds a crowd of youths had gathered round asking me questions, mainly as to why I had cut off my locks.

'Christians don' have locks,' I told them for the umpteenth time.

'Don't ya go wiv girls no more, then,' asked a cheeky white boy.

'An' don' you smoke weed no more?' another asked.

'No more Blues?'

'Don't you rave?'

The questions came thick and fast, and it seemed to me they were only concerned with what I didn't do, rather than what I now did do.

'Look, I'm a Christian now, an' with Jesus in my life, for the first time I know I have something worth livin' for.' I felt the urge welling up in me again to speak out boldly. 'I gave my life to Jesus because he is the only one who can save people, an' he showed me I needed savin'. He's changed me. You better believe I'm diff'rent, an' it's not just that I don' rave no more, it's cos I've got Jesus in me in the inside.'

The crowd was silent. Shocked. Drinking in my words in a kind of mystified stupor. I left them staring after me and wheeled into the pub next door where I knew there would be a good chance I would find Bones, George and one or two other old friends. Randolph was with them round a snooker table.

When I walked in, the game stopped. Then Bones recognised me, and waltzed up to me holding out his hands to shake.

'Was 'appened?' It was the inevitable appeal when old friends saw me without my locks.

'I'm a Christian now.' The inevitable reply.

George began to laugh, but a quick sideways glance at him from me, not with any venom, silenced the chuckling.

I talked to them for about an hour, again holding their attention while I spoke virtually uninterrupted apart from the oldd exclamation of disbelief by one of the three youths. I told them how Jesus was really alive and interested in them, just as he had proved his concern for me. I told them how anyone who turns to Christ is received and forgiven and how, no matter how bad a person he is, God still loves them. Bones blinked with amazement at these words, remembering the almost futile search that had resulted in the long talk just a few months before. Only now it seemed that I had found a reality that outshone his religious interest in Catholicism.

As I walked home that evening, I prayed under my breath for the old friends I had talked to. I felt as though they no longer were close the way they had been, but that didn't matter because now I had a higher calling, and it was to introduce them to Christ. I had obeyed part of that calling by talking to them, and now I prayed for them fervently.

12: Into battle

I realised my friendship with Bones was disintegrating the day my chum said to me: 'I'm goin' ravin'. Let's go to the club, man.' I just knew that wasn't the place for me. The two of us who had walked and talked about finding God were no longer on the same road together. But even though we were heading for different places, I still tried to talk to Bones as much as possible about the Lord, and although there was not the wholehearted response I was looking for, Bones would always listen.

Into the gap left by Bones came Davison. I needed a friend, and once the false image of being slightly mad had been shattered, Davison fitted the bill well. He was an enthusiastic Christian, and he believed in the reality of God in the world. His church, a somewhat wild West Indian church in Harringey, was the scene of our reunion.

I had been invited to a convention at the West Indian church, and I had revelled in the novelty of being asked to go to a church on a Saturday night instead of a club. As soon as I walked through the door I was Davison, and the excitement I felt at seeing him again after such a long break and in the light of being a fellow Christian triggered off the new friendship. Here was a face from the past who would understand and be able to help.

We talked at length, and didn't stop while I gave Davison a lift home in my tatty Cortina. It transpired that at Davison's church there was a series of special meetings aimed at making a real impact on the godlessness of the area. On the Monday night of the convention, I met Davison at the church after work and he introduced me to Mike.

'This is Mike, a friend of mine,' said Davison. 'He can't keep quiet.'

And Davison was quite right, because in Mike there was an uncontrollable fire that motivated him to tell everyone and anyone about Jesus Christ.

The three of us laughed and joked together as I drove the battered Cortina through North London's busy streets. Life was fresh and new, there was an expectancy about every day, and I was enjoying it in a way I had never experienced before.

The car slowed to a crawl in a line of heavy traffic. On the pavement opposite was a long queue waiting for an early evening showing of the latest film, and for a while we studied the faces of couples and families waiting for their tickets.

Mike, something of a home-movie buff, was the first to speak.

'These people need Jesus,' he said. We grunted in agreement. Then light dawned on Mike's face.

'Hey, why don't we get a projector and fine somewhere to show Christian films?'

That suggestion brought a positive response. Davison shifted in the front passenger seat as the idea arrested his keen opportunist mind. Surely this was an ideal way of reaching a generation that was being conditioned to watch and believe. But believe what? The trash and junk of a materialistic society, and the corruption of evil minds. Now was the time to let truth prevail.

'But we've got to pray,' said Mike. 'We can't just go and do this thing without prayer, 'cos it just won't work.'

'Yeah, you're right,' Davison chipped in. 'We should fast and pray.'

The words took me by surprise. Fast? Did he mean not eat? And for how long? I was quiet for a moment while the other two tossed the idea back and forth. Then I heard Davison talking about praying all night, and suddenly I saw there was to be a personal cost if I was to see successful evangelism.

'You mean, we're goin' to eat nothin' and pray all night?' I inquired.

'Sure,' replied Davison.

'You'll be OK,' Mike reassured me, 'it doesn't seem long

when you really get down to prayin', and this is important, man.'

I felt better. Reassured. I didn't know how I could cope because I had never gone for long without food and sleep, and I admitted to myself that I had been finding a deep, inner satisfaction in praying intensely for long periods.

'I reckon it should be three days,' said Davison, and that was agreed. Three days and three nights fasting, and praying through one night.

Well, I've been to all-night Blues, so why not all-night praying? I thought.

But where? We tried to find a house or a room somewhere where we could be undisturbed and not annoy anyone by our unusual action. Eventually, we settled on an unlikely solution: Lemina, my sister, agreed, mainly because she wanted to go out late at night and here were three ready-made babysitters for her two small children.

'You sure?' I asked, inquisitive because Lemina was not usually so readily sympathetic to my antics. She was sure. The fast would begin on Thursday night and go through to Sunday. The all-night praying would take place on Saturday night. The aim – to become more effective witnesses in telling people about Jesus, particularly with a view to using Christian films. We meant business.

It was Saturday evening. I felt weak. I noticed that the other two looked fighting fit, with no visible signs of fatigue or hunger. How do they do it, I thought.

We sang some songs, and that made me feel good inside. It wrenched my attention away from luring mental picture of well-laden platters, and forced me to concentrate on worshipping God.

'He is Lord,' we sang. 'He is risen from the dead, and he is Lord.'

My spirit soared, and food didn't matter so much now.

'Every knee shall bow, every tongue confess, that Jesus Christ is Lord.'

I raised my hands, now oblivious to any hunger, and the action of lifting my arms in this way was now automatic, the humorous picture of Pastor Perry praying with his hands raised was now long forgotten. This was the way to worship God, and I revelled in it.

We prayed. On our knees, sitting, standing. We implored God to use us, to fill us with more supernatural power. We laughed. We cried. We remained silent and we shouted. And before I even thought to look at my watch the early hours had come and outside the dawn chorus had struck up.

I was amazed at the stamina, both physical and spiritual, of these two young men, and then I reminded myself that I had gone along all the way with them. I glowed inside and wondered if God was pleased with me, allowing myself a luxurious moment of pride. Surely, God must be pleased?

Suddenly I was shaken and heard a voice saying, 'Les, you awake?' Sheepishly, I realised I had dropped off to sleep, and I was embarrassed.

'It's OK,' said Davison, 'I dropped off too.'

And the next thing I knew it was nine o'clock, and I had slept right through for three hours from six a.m., totally exhausted. When I awoke, I saw that the other two were asleep, and they looked as though nothing would stir them.

I stretched, and headed for the kitchen. 'It's over,' I thought. I put Lemina's kettle on and, on the spur of the moment, I decided to cook three platefuls of eggs, beefburgers and anything else I could find to end our fast on a happy note. A real break-fast.

The sizzling beefburgers failed to wake the others, while the smell drove me crazy and made my taste-buds scream uncontrollably. Finally the meal was prepared, and with a large tray laden with breakfast I stepped into the living-room.

'Here it is,' I announced proudly.

'Enjoy it,' said Davison, rubbing sleep from his eyes and at the same time looking at his watch.

'We're fasting until after church tonight.'

I stared open-eyed, looking at Davison then to my trayful of goodies, and back to Davison again.

'It's OK, you carry on,' said Mike, now awake and showing no signs of succumbing to the lavish temptation. 'Don't mind us.'

That Sunday morning I ate three breakfasts and still had room for more!

13: Seeing is believing

Exciting days had come for Mike, Davison and me. We knew that, following our intense praying, God was going to use us in a different and tremendous way through this ministry that was unfolding.

I had begun a job as a dark-room technician. As an eighteen-year-old, I was learning a new trade in photography, and longed for more adventure as a Fleet Street photographer. But my job took second place to my new-found mission of reaching other people for the Lord Jesus Christ. Even the pulsating excitement of standing on the touch line at a first division match at Highbury and seeing the great stars in action did not grip me as much as my desire to share the good news that Jesus Christ was alive and working in the world today.

Mike, in his early twenties, and his new wife, Joelle, had just had their first baby. They were still living at Mike's mother's home and were waiting for a council house. Davison, also in his early twenties, had embarked on a training scheme to learn engineering.

The three of us realised that a projector would cost something approaching £200. We had to find the money, which would be a difficult task, but not impossible – and indeed, to God a very small matter. We firmly believed the Lord was leading us to set up a film-showing enterprise and therefore he was going to provide everything we needed. We agreed between ourselves that we were quite willing to make any sacrifice in this cause.

The pastor at Davison's pentecostal church in Harringey was excited when he heard about our venture. At the next possible opportunity, he announced in a church meeting what Davison, Mike and I were up to, and asked for a special offering to be taken up. That day the church gave more than £100 in one collection on a Sunday morning for the film-showing work. Before we knew it, we had our projector, brand new, sparkling and full of complicated knobs and buttons just waiting to be used to show people the way to God.

Mike took it upon himself to be the one responsible for hiring films from organisations such as Don Summers and International Films. I used my influence from former days to set up film shows in numerous youth clubs around London. I enjoyed going back and meeting old friends and arranging for the special evenings that were to change many people's lives.

Many of the youth leaders at the clubs were overjoyed. They begged me to arrange the film showings as quickly as possible, for many of them were at their wits' end in trying to improve the lives of the young people in their clubs. Anything that gave a glimmer of hope that things could get better was jumped at. Some even said, 'If the boys and girls are converted, that's a welcome relief for us, and it will be a great help.' They were crying out for help that was now being offered in the form of our mission of faith.

The film roadshow was fully booked in no time. Sometimes seven evenings a week were taken up going to homes, churches, youth clubs – anywhere where people were prepared to sit down in large or small groups and watch a film. Even the sequence was worked out miraculously by the Lord. The films we hired just seemed to fit the venues we went to, and many, many people were spoken to and their lives touched through this medium.

It wasn't long before the film ministry was in big demand all over London, north, south, east and west. We discovered people were very enthusiastic about watching a film, much more so than listening to a preacher. The tried and trusted custom of putting on special church meetings with a guest speaker would bring only a handful of people out of a hundred invited. But it was different with film shows, mainly because we were taking the message to the people in their own environment, in their homes and in the youth clubs.

I was motivated very much by a passage of Scripture in

the book of James upon which I meditated frequently. There I read that faith without works is dead. I had exercised the faith in prayer and fasting, but now was the time for action, and the action was proving successful. In people's homes it was not unusual for an entire family to come to the Lord and give their hearts to Jesus Christ, surrendering their wills to him and pledging to serve him with their lives.

I found great liberty in summing up after a film show, particularly in people's homes. I would tell them: 'God is not like the telephone operator. Sometimes you just cannot get hold of the operator when you dial 100. The phone keeps ringing and ringing and ringing. Sometimes they answer, sometimes there is a long wait. But it is different with God – you talk to him and he's always there, ready and listening, able to help, and there is never any delay with him.'

After talking like this, on many occasions, parents and children alike would surrender their lives to God, often in floods of tears. Mike and Davison and I would pray with them, and invariably they would say afterwards how different they felt inside.

One day we were walking in north London outside a further education college when we met a sixteen-year-old West Indian. He was big for his age, muscular and fit-looking.

'We are Christians and we are talking to people about God,' was my bland opening. The youth looked at me with a startled expression.

'Hey, man, we're not Bible bashers,' I reassured him. 'But we just want to share something special with you. If I could open you up and put the word of God into you to make you realise what we mean, I would. But I know I can't do it like that.'

The youth by now had recovered his composure. 'Say, you're a bit strange, but you might as well tell me some more.'

After ten minutes of gentle persuasion and explaining the good news, I offered to pray for the youth. He agreed. When we had finished praying, the sixteen-year-old, who towered above even my bulky, six-foot frame, threw his arms around Mike and me, pulled us to his side and said, 'Man, I feel great.' As he said 'great', he squeezed and lifted the two of us from the ground. Then he let us go and jumped up and down for joy.

'God is real,' was his exclamation as he realised the truth of what had been told him.

That evening, at about ten p.m., Mike, Davison, I and some other Christians were packed into a van to pray for the youth and other people we had contacted that day. I was crushed into a corner in the back of the van near the door. The praying was intense and rather noisy, and at times the van would rock with the enthusiasm of praying young people.

I looked up and saw a blue helmet through the back window. Then I noticed blue lights flashing, bringing my sudden and now unnecessary reaction of old back to life. I scrambled to my feet, treading on several other people at the same time, regaining my composure as I wiped away the condensation on the inside of the window, and saw two Black Marias and a police panda car.

I opened the doors to be confronted by several policemen, shutting the van doors behind me to allow the praying to continue.

'What are you doing?' said one of the policemen in a gruff voice.

'We're praying.' I said the statement in a matter-of-fact way, not cockily, but meekly. The burly policemen were stunned into silence. They looked into the van through the steamy windows with wide eyes to see not drug taking, not drunken revelling but well-behaved young people. They felt sheepish.

I said, 'We were just talking to our Saviour. He means so much to us, and we love talking to him about everything we do.'

The policemen looked at each other.

'I mean, Jesus loves you too, you know?' I went on.

'Yes, I know that, sonny, but we've had complaints about you and you'd better move on.'

'Certainly, officer,' I said. 'But first can we give you these tracts that will tell you why we love talking to Jesus.' The policemen looked reluctant so I pressed home the point.

'You can read them later if you want but please take them because we want you to understand what has happened to us. We want to tell as many people as possible that there is a new way to live, and it is a tremendous life.'

'That may well be, sonny, but you had better move on.' The policemen were beginning to look rather menacing. So I thrust out a handful of tracts, and breathed a sigh of relief as a big hairy hand took them. I climbed back in through the back doors of the van, and announced, 'It's OK, let's go,' and we moved on.

By now, a team of young people was forming around our enthusiastic mission. We would frequently concentrate on one area if we felt a good response there to what we were saying. If people showed an eagerness to know more, our team of young people would move into the area and witness on the streets for about a week. We capitalised on the spiritual response that we could identify in different areas.

Many youth club leaders were crying out for the team to return. They were struggling to deal with delinquents and disturbed young people from broken homes. They were desperate for any help they could get, and a lot of youth club leaders were constantly in touch with me asking us to come back.

I would get home from work in the evening, rush my evening meal, and be off out straight away to meet Davison and Mike to go on to youth clubs or wherever we had been invited. It was hard work and very tiring.

During a week-long mission in Hackney, the team went to five youth clubs on different evenings of the week, plus a school youth club, using the film *The Cross and the Switchblade*. When we arrived at the school and began unloading our equipment from the car, boys and girls would rush up and demand to know what was going on, with an enthusiastic expectation. They were hoping for excitement to dispel some of the boredom they were experiencing.

'I hope it's not one of those boring films,' the pupils would say.

'How much is it going to cost us?' was another frequent question.

And the answer would always come back, 'It's free'. We never charged for film shows but trusted God to provide all the money we needed. The fact that it was free seemed to bring a startling response from the schoolchildren, who were not used to getting something for nothing.

Once the projector and screen had been set up in the school hall, we would concentrate on getting the youth into the hall, seated and ready and listening. I would frequently be the one to rise to my feet to explain what was going to happen.

'After the film, we are going to talk to you about Jesus,' I would say. At that point came jeers and shouts, but I knew that during the film opinions about Jesus Christ would begin to change.

I prayed out loud before each film was shown, briefly to avoid too much heckling from the irreligious young people. Then the film started. And with the film there always came a dramatic change of attitude, with the viewers caught up with the challenge of what happened to the aggressive gangs in New York when God met with them.

At the end of the film show I would stand up to speak again. And it was on these occasions I found that what happened to Dave Wilkerson, the man behind *The Cross and the Switchblade*, happened to me also. The ring leaders in the audience would mock me with taunts like, 'Hey, preach, you gonna take up the offering now?' It made speaking very difficult, and I learned to take authority in the way Dave Wilkerson learned.

'All right, I'm going to speak and you're going to listen,' I would say. And the firmness in my voice, coupled with the fire in my eyes, would arrest the young people and get their attention.

At the school in Hackney I spoke for about fifteen minutes. I spoke words I had not intended to speak and felt the power of the Holy Spirit welling up within me.

The audience listened intently and I knew I was getting through to them.

When I had finished speaking, I said, 'Now we are going to pray.' This time there was more reverence. And when I had finished praying, I added, 'Is there anyone here tonight who really wants to know the Lord Jesus Christ?'

I looked at the large audience of young people, and noticed that some were deep in thought while some were looking at their friends for their reaction. Some were embarrassed and some were afraid to do anything for fear of what their friends would think. But when I asked for a show of hands, some responded. Excited, I invited those who wanted to give their lives to Christ to talk to me and the other members of the team afterwards, and we would pray with any who needed help. After we had packed up all the equipment, Davison and I each had a group of inquisitive young people talking with us outside the school. After a few minutes, the youth leader ran up to the group and singled me out.

'God sent you here,' he said, with tears welling in his eyes. 'God sent you, I know. I can see God is in you, because I'm a backslider and I know how to recognise when God is at work.'

We were there until eleven-thirty that night talking for hours on end with young people hungry for God. The following night we went to another youth club – but this one was different.

It was a black youth club where Rastafarianism was rife – full of young people with their dreadlocks and their ganja, either converts to the fast-rising cult or thinking about becoming Rastafarians.

There was a common attitude that the Church had exploited black people along with the white races, and the issue was very sensitive. Anyone seen to be joining the white man's religion was regarded with, at the least, suspicion, and at the most hatred.

Out of that meeting came an invitation to speak at a youth club in Acton, another Rastafarian club run by black-belt karate experts who were the youth leaders. I took the team with me, and on arrival a bearded West Indian with long dreadlocks looked menacingly at us and said, 'What you comin' here for with your white man's God?' That was the challenge laid down – could Christianity with its essentially Western reputation meet the needs of West Indians and other ethnic groups with their partly justified persecution complex?

I found during that evening that a lot of the members of the youth club were in fact backsliders from evangelical Christianity. They had been Christians but had left their churches and now were attracted by Rastafarianism. Three of the youths there were particularly abusive and swore repeatedly at me and the team. One of them, the ring leader, was short and stocky, with long locks, and very aggressive. Before the meeting this ring leader squared up to me and looked as though he wanted to pick a fight. I felt fear trying to take over my life. I felt the adrenalin flow, just like in the old days, and instinctively my hands curled into iron-like fists ready for action. But as we eyed each other, both giving and meeting a challenge of strength, I felt that new-found love of God well up in my heart, and a strong faith begin to replace the feelings of aggression that were inside.

It was a supernatural faith, because I knew it was not my basic nature to consider such a challenge a spritual rather than a physical attack. But I was on enemy territory, and the Lord was with me. I had been sent on a divine mission, and the opponent I now faced was loved by God as much as I was loved by God, and the opposition I faced came not from this burly, short, mean-looking West Indian but from Satan himself.

The challenge came to nothing, and after that evening's film show the Rastafarian ring leader was no longer so aggressive, but even came up to me and threw his arms around me repeating: 'Love, man, love . . .'

Some people in that youth club were responsive to the good news presented to them that night, while others remained hostile. But whatever the reaction, God had been at work – and I knew that bad reaction, although preferably coupled with good reaction was far better than no reaction at all.

In the churches that invited the film roadshow, there was an encouraging reaction. We mainly showed films that inspired the Christians there and prompted a deeper commitment to Christ. Frequently we would go into a church that had become introspective or defeated in its attitude, and build their faith to the point where the church moved on, ready to get into spiritual warfare and begin to see positive results. As a team of young Christians, we inspired people by our raw enthusiasm, and testified to the move of God in the streets of London near where the people in these churches lived. We asked for prayer and received the backing of ministers and their churches who would pledge to intercede for us in our special and unique work.

Many church leaders and pastors would say, 'Come back soon and tell us more.' And there were frequently people giving their hearts to the Lord Jesus Christ as my friends and I spoke of miracle-working faith in God.

In one Tottenham church we showed a film made for Easter celebrations about the Crucifixion and Resurrection. In the audience was a Rastafarian. After the film show he came and talked with me and explained how he had been touched and moved by what he had seen. He poured out his heart, displaying deep inner needs that could not be met by Rastafarianism, and revealed his disillusionment with the cult. He gave his heart to the Lord, and that night embarked on a new life that has since led him to Bible College and successful Christian work in a south London church.

14: Truth to tell

My friends and I frequently went to parks in the summer and were always ready to tell somebody about our new life in Christ. We took advantage of the long summer evenings to wander in the parks in north London looking for people with time on their hands who were ready to listen.

On one occasion we came across a group of about twenty-five youths, boys and girls, who stood out as the perfect opportunity for spreading the good news. Mike and I approached the gang.

'Excuse me,' I said to the nearest youth, 'we are Christians, and wondered if you have got ten minutes to spare because we would like to talk to you.'

The youth eyed Mike and me suspiciously. Some of the others nearby stopped what they were doing and turned to look at us, while others in the group carried on chatting, laughing and joking.

'OK,' said the youth. 'You can talk to us. What is it that you want?'

Mike replied, 'We want to tell you about the Lord Jesus Christ.'

With that most of the youths went quiet and focused their attention on us. They were still suspicious.

'We have discovered that life without Jesus Christ is empty and meaningless,' Mike went on. 'We have committed our lives to Christ and he has made such a tremendous difference that we wanted to tell you about it.' Some of the youths laughed, but others listened intently.

'Yeah, and we also have found that serving Jesus is not dull and boring,' I chipped in. 'It's an exciting way of life, and we have been totally changed by the love of God.'

While Mike and I shared with the youths some of the older ones began to get annoyed. One of them, quite evidently the leader of the group, walked up to me and swore in my face.

'Push off,' he said aggressively. The rest of the group began to be agitated and it crossed our minds that we were in for trouble. The more we spoke about Jesus the more angry the older youths got. Then some of them bent to the ground and picked up stones or any near object and were apparently about to chase us off.

Some of the older West Indians began to hit the stones they had picked up on the side of a park bench, making a rhythm, while at the same time staring angrily at us all. The stones crashing rhythmically on the wooden bench were a warning being sounded that the gang was in an aggressive mood and we got the message. We tried to speak louder over the din of the drumming, but the more we spoke the more anger and irritation was expressed by the gang.

We moved off, and some of the gang who had been interested followed us, wanting to talk some more: For three hours we shared what we knew about the Lord Jesus Christ with those who were interested, and after listening one or two of them said they wanted to become Christians. But during the whole time there were frequent interruptions from the other youths who were always in the background, and always seeking to make their presence felt.

The next evening Mike and I went back to the same park, and the same spot, where we spoke to about fifteen of the youths. We were there until it got dark, sharing the reality of our experience and answering questions. Most of the youths were scared to make any kind of commitment, because they didn't want to be seen by the rest of the gang and were frightened of being ridiculed or outcast by their friends. But three of them committed their lives to Christ, kneeling in the park with us and asking Jesus Christ into their hearts.

The following evening Mike and I again found success as we shared the gospel with any who would listen. We led people to Christ in the street. We prayed there, in the full view of passers-by, ignoring the funny looks, leading people into the kingdom of God. I had decided that it didn't matter to me if anyone thought I was made. I was going to do whatever God told me to do, and if that meant kneeling to pray in the street, then so be it. God's work was more important than what men thought. Young people coming into the kingdom of God and starting completely new lives was the vital issue of the day, not anybody's reputation.

We frequently puzzled and prayed over how to reach more people. We counted up and realised that by talking to groups of youths in parks and on street corners, we were reaching hundreds of people, but we were dissatisfied and wanted to tell more people about the Lord. So it was not long before someone suggested a newspaper or a magazine. We agreed we could produce a monthly newsletter full of testimony to the power of Jesus Christ and the work of the Holy Spirit today and send it around the streets near where we lived.

But to do it we needed printing equipment, and once again we were faced with an exercise of faith to bring in expensive equipment. We decided that nothing but the best equipment was needed, but that would be expensive. We agreed on a good-quality duplicator in order to be able to print newsletters to send around homes in north London.

I got in touch with a firm that supplied duplicators, and they sent a representative to see me. That was the moment when I realised that anything up to a thousand pounds would be needed. And we didn't have a penny.

We reminded ourselves that we were similarly placed when looking for film-showing equipment, and agreed together that our God was well able to provide a printing machine. Within a few weeks we had a duplicator.

I sold my large four-year-old Ford Consul to raise some of the money and others made similar sacrifices. Coupled with gifts we raised the money. We also were given an electric typewriter, a gift from someone who heard about the evangelistic work we were doing. Money rolled in, enough to keep us supplied with everything we needed to do the things that God was showing us to do.

We agreed to call the magazine *Lifeline*, and help in producing it came in the form of Joan, from a church in Mitcham, who was to be editor. Then there was Sonia from Haringey who would type and produce stencils for the duplicated newsletter.

We sent the new *Lifeline* newsletter to about 700 homes over a few months and it proved to be a tremendous success. The magazine informed people of what was being arranged by the team in the way of evangelistic meetings and film shows. It was quite clear that God was behind this magazine and, however amateurish it appeared, people recognised that the living God was behind it.

The Lord saw we were willing young people and every day he took us deeper into a new dimension of life. And the more we discovered of God and his love, the more people were born again into the kingdom of God. Our lives were filled with constant joy because others were finding the Saviour for themselves.

Everything we needed was provided. The projector and film equipment was just the beginning. The duplicator was just another item in the long list of miracles that were handed out to us by a loving God. I needed to replace the car I sold because prayer groups in Luton and even as far away as Bedford were clamouring for life. And that car was provided for me! Money for vital literature such as tracts and books also came in.

One gift of books came from a bookshop in south west London. I had spoken to the manager about the work in which I was involved, and the manager promised he would pray for our evangelism. Two weeks later there came a phone call from someone who had been in the bookshop and spoken to the manager, and thirty-six copies of *The Cross and the Switchblade* and its sequel *Run Baby Run* were provided for the outreach.

My friends and I were greatly encouraged by the miracles that happened day by day. The more God moved the more we held all-night prayer meetings, sometimes in our homes, sometimes in a car, or in someone's home in another part of the country. We realised prayer was the key to success, and when we prayed we believed that God would give us more of his power to be effective witnesses for Christ, and that our Christian lives would become more fruitful.

15: Jamaica

I always wanted to go back to the West Indies. And my chance came when Davison's pastor announced he was going to Jamaica to hold a mission in Montego Bay. I found myself totally taken up by the idea of going with Pastor Franklin.

In my heart I determined to be on that trip. My chance to go back to the West Indies appeared to have arrived, but instead of going for a holiday, as I thought I would go, here was my chance to go and serve the Lord with a team of other Christians.

Pastor Franklin announced that he wanted to take others with him to work in Montego Bay and make the mission a success. But there were obstacles in the way to prevent me going. It would cost money, lots of it, and it would mean taking time off work. I got down to serious prayer and again put my faith into action and believed that I would be on that trip. I talked to Pastor Franklin who agreed that I should go to Jamaica with him.

Special offerings were taken up towards the fares of the fourteen people who would be going, including Mike and myself, for quite a number of young people had felt God leading them to go on the trip. Through offerings, the church was prepared to pay half of my fare and I agreed to pay half myself.

Because I had to take time off work to go, I had to fly out separately from the rest of the team. I could not leave work until a week after the others had left, and I was to fly out to join them. There was no flight available any earlier, so I had to resign myself to missing the first part of the month-long mission. The flight would be eight hours to Bermuda, and then another two hours to Jamaica.

I boarded the plane. My seat was next to that of a young

woman, and I realised that I would be sitting next to her for eight hours and therefore would have plenty of opportunity to talk to her about the Lord.

I looked around. Here was an expensive piece of machinery that man had made, machinery that could fly in the air, complicated and skilfully made. God had given man wisdom to make such equipment. I marvelled at God's generosity and mercy in giving so much to man when man had so continually rejected God and had turned his back on him.

On take-off I instinctively knew that something was wrong. I looked out of the porthole where I could see two of the four engines. Just by looking at the engines I knew one of them was not working. When the aircraft landed in Bermuda the captain announced, 'Ladies and gentlemen, due to a fault in one of the engines we will have to stay in Bermuda for a few hours.'

I knew that one of the engines had been at fault but God had brought us safely across the ocean. The airline put all the passengers in a four-star hotel in Bermuda to wait out the time it took to repair the engine.

While at the hotel I began to get to know some of the people who were involuntarily staying on the island with me. For each meal I sat at the same table with the same eight people who were on their way to Jamaica. Included among them was the girl I had spoken to on the flight, a Scottish teacher going to Jamaica to take up her first job. Among the people I met were those visiting Jamaica to see relatives and people flying out to take up new jobs. Everyone seemed to be waiting for something, waiting for what they did not know. I knew I would have to speak sooner or later, because I was incapable of keeping quiet when I knew that what I had in my life would be attractive to those who were waiting for their journey to continue.

'Excuse me,' I began, 'but I am Christian and before we eat dinner tonight I would like to give thanks for the food that God has provided for us, because in this world there are millions of people starving while we have what we need. Do you mind if I pray before we begin our meal?'

For a moment the people at the table in the hotel

restaurant blinked and stared at me. Then they bowed their heads and waited for me to pray.

'Heavenly Father, I thank you for providing this food for us. We are grateful for all that you give to us, in Jesus' name, Amen.' I was nervous, uncertain what sort of reaction I would get, but I went through with it in deep gratitude to God for his provision.

After the prayer I overheard one of them say, 'It's a long time since I have said grace at table.'

A young West Indian, who by his accent gave away that his home was in north London, asked me why I was so religious. I explained that it was not so much a question of being religious, but that I had found reality in the Lord Jesus Christ, and had discovered that Christ was personal and was pleased when people spoke to him, even about the little things in life.

No one, surprisingly, was offended by my action. Instead, people seemed to be moved and touched and even convicted by what I had done. A long and involved conversation followed, prompted by searching questions. Everyone was involved in the conversation that night about the Lord Jesus Christ.

By the next day the engine had been fixed, and the journey could continue. The flight across vast expanses of green-blue Atlantic Ocean took us to Kingston, the capital of Jamaica. The plane touched down at six-thirty in the morning and from there I took an internal flight to Montego Bay on the northern shore of Jamaica.

The airport was full of hustling porters, all offering their services.

'Can ah take you bag, sah,' they would say. All eager for easy pickings in tips, and concentrating mainly on those who looked to be better-off.

Once out of the airport in Montego Bay, I drank in everything I could about my new environment. I was back in the West Indies. Back in the islands from which I came. I was shocked at the marked difference between rich and poor – the poor were so poor they were easily identifiable from the rich who were wealthy enough to drive around in the best cars and looked immaculate in their smart clothes.

I took a cab, which coughed into life and headed off into the haze, great drops of sweat dangling from the ears of the driver like grotesque, glistening ear-rings, before splashing on to his stained shirt. Then we wheeled back into the shanty town, heading for the address on the piece of paper I had thrust into the driver's hand.

There seemed to be many street-side markets laden with luscious fruit, bananas yellower than I had seen in London, and water melons stacked in enormous piles.

It was Sunday. I was supposed to have arrived the previous day, but owing to the delay I was a day late. As the taxi sped towards its destination, I was amazed to be feeling so much at home. I didn't feel 5,500 miles from home. I felt good, and I was overjoyed at the sights that greeted my eyes.

At one time I felt I was in heaven, because most people seemed to be dressed in white, wearing simple headgear, and all carrying their Bibles as they made their way to church. Every hundred yards there seemed to be a church building, and although the address to which I had been told to go was built as a house, it was used as a church. When I got there I was greeted by some of the team who came running out to meet me and to take me to the place where I was to stay.

The angelic sound of singing and clapping could be heard, people singing praises to God. The sound went so well with the calm deep-green sea and the cloudless blue sky. This surely must be God's land, I mistakenly thought.

That evening, having taken my luggage to the flat where I was staying and caught up on some sleep, I went with the team to the church where that evening's mission was to be held. When I arrived, there were already people sitting around outside the church, which surprisingly was only half built. There were parts of the building missing, and I could see that there were at least 200 crammed inside.

The service that evening lasted two hours. Pastor Franklin seemed to be motivated by the occasion and his message was greeted by an enthusiastic response with people giving their hearts to Christ.

That night I again slept deeply. I was woken up the next morning by singing, the sound of young children on their way to school:

Well I'll see you in the rapture,
O see you in the rapture,
I'll see you in the meeting in the air,
And with my blessed Saviour,
We'll sing and reign for ever,
I'll see you in the meeting in the air.

I smiled, and thought how God was so integrally a part of the way of life in Jamaica. People were singing everywhere. I felt glad to be alive, and happy to be in Jamaica. I pulled on my sawn-off jeans and T-shirt, thrust back the curtains and looked out of the window. I saw the children on their way to school, wearing their bright uniforms, skipping together down the dusty track towards the town.

I took a walk into town, and it was during this trip to look around my new environment that I realised that I wasn't in heaven after all. I saw a young policeman, no more than twenty-one years old, talking to two youths, one of them wearing long Rastafarian locks, the other with a less distinctive appearance. The policeman appeared to be harassing the two youths. He was thrusting his authority on to them for no apparent reason, and for a moment I feared the policeman was about to make use of the ugly-looking revolver strapped at his side. Later I learned that in Jamaica it was not uncommon for youths, trouble-makers, or just possible troublemakers, to be gunned down where they stood. The islands had a record of numerous shootings and there was a law of shoot or be shot.

I determined in my heart that this island needed to hear about God, and I was going to waste no time in bringing the good news of salvation, playing my part to the full.

That evening there was another service, and again there were not only hundreds crammed into the building, but hundreds outside also. While Pastor Franklin spoke to the crowd inside some of the team members went outside to speak to the people who couldn't get in.

That evening I counselled two young girls who had gone to the front of the church to respond to an appeal made by Pastor Franklin. As I talked to them about the love of God, one of them broke down in tears, and they both surrendered their lives to Christ to serve him. The following evening I saw them both again, and was delighted when it became apparent that what they had experienced was real and life-changing.

Every day, and from one church to the next, people's lives were transformed by the power of God's word. We witnessed to people on the streets, and I found myself talking to more and more Rastafarians. I was amazed that in a place like Jamaica where there seemed to be so many churches, there were also so many Rastafarians. Was it because this was an island full of people searching for truth? If so, then some were finding themselves getting into deception rather than the truth of the Lord Jesus Christ.

One day I found myself speaking to an intelligent Rastafarian, whom I asked 'What do you think about Jesus?'

'I believe in him,' said the Rastafarian thoughtfully.

'Why don't you go to church, and why aren't you a Christian then?' I asked.

In the conversation that ensued I discovered that the Rastafarian had been brought up by Christian parents, but had never had an experience of his own of the Lord Jesus Christ. He did not know the truth for himself, and had been depending on the experience of his parents instead. But this youth wanted to find out more about God, and sadly no one had shown him the way.

Another Rastafarian youth with whom I spoke announced, 'I am God. I and I is God.' (God is in me so I am God.)

'What about Selassie?' I asked, wanting to find out what Rastafarians thought of the man they had worshipped now that he was dead.

'Selassie? Just a man,' came the reply. 'I don't believe in him. Some dread believes in him, but I, man, over dat.' (I am now passed believing that Selassie is God.)

Another Rastafarian told me, 'Man, there are so many hypocrites in the Church, so I jus' left.'

I assured him, 'Oh yes, there are hypocrites in the Church, but God has never failed us. He is God. I might fail you, and I might be a hypocrite, and the Church could fail you, but God never fails.'

I realised that the reason why there were so many Rastafarians in Jamaica was that many young people had rebelled against the Church for distinctive reasons. They needed something to worship, and something to cling on to, and Rastafarianism had proved the alternative. Encouraged by reggae heroes such as Bob Marley, they had been egged on into the new cult. Jamaicans had never been a people to do away with religion, and if one system failed they would find another. They were a people who recognised their need for God, and they mistakenly thought they had the answers in Rastafarianism. Even if it meant worshipping a man, or even the cult of self, Jamaicans would find a spiritual object of worship in some form or other.

That was where Selassie had come in, with his appeal to the roots of black West Indians. He had been proclaimed the answer to the search for peace and the inner longing to go to Africa and live in a land without policemen and without laws. They wanted to be free from harassment, either from uniformed policemen or from white people, and they wanted to be themselves. They wanted to do just what they liked, without being interfered with. And they had lost sight of the liberty that Jesus Christ offered them.

Each day the evangelistic team from London held evening meetings, parades down town, open-air meetings and witnessing on the streets. We visited schools and shared the life of Christ with the children. Here I found that, unlike England, we could preach the gospel in schools and invite the children to respond, leading them to Christ and encouraging them to go to church and become strong Christians.

I remembered how boring I had found assembly when I was at school, and determined that whenever I spoke at school assemblies I would either have the attention of the children to whom I was speaking, or I would not bother. I enjoyed the responsive attitudes I found among the Jamaican children, and I and the other team members felt a great liberty in proclaiming the gospel in the schools on the island.

16: The fire

> While Apollos was in Corinth, Paul made his way overland as far as Ephesus, where he found a number of disciples. When he asked, 'Did you receive the Holy Spirit when you became believers?' they answered, 'No, we were never even told there was such a thing as a Holy Spirit.' 'Then how were you baptised?' he asked. 'With John's baptism,' they replied. 'John's baptism,' said Paul, 'was a baptism of repentance; but he insisted that the people should believe in the one who was to come after him – in other words Jesus.' When they heard this they were baptised in the name of the Lord Jesus, and the moment Paul had laid hands on them, the Holy Spirit came down on them, and they began to speak with tongues and to prophesy. There were about twelve of these men (Acts 19. 1–7 (Jerusalem Bible)).

I loved going to London's parks to witness for Jesus. Somehow talking to people under a clear blue sky, among trees and plants, made me feel freer in my spirit, and I often felt the freshness of God's Holy Spirit moving through me like a gentle breeze.

But there were times when something else stirred deep down inside me. Fear. At first I tried to dismiss it, but it nagged at my mind – wasn't the Lord of life living in me? What had I to fear? Yet it was there, none-the-less.

Rastas grow their hair into dreadlocks with the set purpose of instilling fear into other people – that's why they are called *dread*locks. One day Mike and I met a group of Rastas in that still twilight you so often find late on summer evenings. It was close, and getting dark. We walked up to them with our usual outward panache, but while talking to them a fear came over me. And without giving away the fact that he knew that fear was in me, Mike sensed there was something wrong.

I thought to myself as we talked to the fearsome looking Rastas: 'How come you are scared, Les? You were a Rasta. What's making you scared now?' I addressed myself inwardly with angry questioning, ashamed that a man of my strength should feel fear.

After speaking to the Rastas for about half an hour, we headed home. As we walked, Mike popped in the inevitable question.

'You were scared, weren't you?'

There was a pause while I looked down at the pavement as we walked. Then I said, 'Yes, I was scared, and I don't know why.' That was all. I was ashamed.

Mike said, 'Man, don't you see, the evil one was over-shadowing you. Fear comes from Satan, not from God. One of the reasons you are feeling this fear is that you are not filled with the Holy Spirit. Do you know what I mean?'

I told Mike I did know what he meant, although I didn't fully understand it. All I knew was that I needed God's strength in me, and without something overwhelmingly powerful motivating me from within, I knew that I would be ineffective as one of God's disciples.

'Do you want to be filled with the Holy Spirit?' asked Mike. His question dragged my thoughts remorselessly back into the present and interrupted my uneasiness about the future.

'You kidding?' I replied. 'That's what I want more than anything else right now.' Somehow I knew that without this gift the future would always remain a problem for me, and the fear would not go away.

The conversation I had with Mike that evening made me more eager than I had ever been to have that gift of the baptism in the Holy Spirit, that extra abundance of power which I knew I needed.

It turned out to be a child who was sent to provide the trigger to set off God's explosion in me. I was standing one evening outside our church building in Vauxhall with a good friend of mind, Sister Gwen, with whom I often spoke about the Holy Spirit and this baptism that I needed. She explained many things to me, and told me the background to the need for this experience. That evening, having just come out of an evening meeting, we bumped into a black woman in her thirties with her nine-year-old daughter. They were looking for a church to go to in the area, having just recently moved house.

The woman, forward but not rude, said to Gwen, 'Sister, you filled with the Holy Spirit?'

'Yes,' replied Gwen.

Then, to my surprise, the child chirped, 'Brother, you filled with the Holy Spirit?'

'No,' I mumbled, shuffling nervously, annoyed at myself for feeling embarrassed about being questioned by a little girl over something I didn't have, and for allowing it to make me feel inadequate.

The girl continued to amaze us both, by explaining, 'It's so simple, brother. God really wants to give you this gift. All you have to do is ask.'

Her words hit home to me harder than anything I had heard before. No one could know better about receiving gifts than a child, and in the simplest terms this girl, with her simple but strong faith, was explaining to me that I need wait no longer. She was supernaturally gifted in a way in which I wish more adults were, and in the five minutes during which we talked, she had been instrumental in helping me to grasp something that even gifted preachers had not fully put across to me.

As suddenly as they appeared, they had gone, hopping cheerily on to a double-decker.

Driving home that evening, giving Gwen a lift, the thoughts provoked by this short conversation were racing round my mind. Gwen was talking to me, but my mind was totally given over to thinking about this baptism of fire.

'You thinking about what that little girl said?' Gwen inquired.

All I could say was, 'Yeah', and that was all.

I had a quick cup of coffee at Gwen's, and drove straight home. In the car I found my mind dwelling on the instances in the New Testament where people were filled with the

Holy Spirit. The words of Acts chapter two came flooding into my mind: 'And suddenly a sound came from heaven like the rush of a mighty wind, and it filled out all the house . . . and there appeared to them tongues as of fire, distributed and resting on each one of them. And they were all filled with the Holy Spirit and began to speak in other tongues, as the Spirit gave them utterance.'

What would it be like to speak in another language without learning it? How could I do the seemingly impossible? Wouldn't I feel a bit stupid? I put these thoughts out of my mind when I remembered the words of Jesus, when he said, 'I will send the Comforter.' And I could almost audibly hear him saying, 'If any man thirst, let him come unto me and drink.'

When I got home, I burst in through the front door, draped my jacket untidily over a chair and, without hesitating, dashed into my room. I dropped to my knees in my bedroom, feeling that exciting pull of the Holy Spirit that I experienced when I knew I had to pray. With the first words, the tears came, uncontrollably and unashamedly running down my face.

'I want to be filled, Lord,' I sobbed. 'I just want to be filled, I want to be filled . . .' I repeated the sentence over and over again.

I was on my knees for twenty minutes crying to the Lord. But still no tongues, and no mystical stirring within.

Mike and Davison were by now taken up with the need that had gripped my imagination, to be filled with the Holy Spirit. One day they told me, 'Les, we are going to pray that God will fill you. We are going to pray and fast for a day, and we are going to believe with you that God is going to do what he promises in his word.' At the end of the day on which they fasted, they came to my home where I was living with my father and brothers and sisters. They prayed with me, and I felt a strong sense of the presence of the Holy Spirit. But still no tongues, and I was still waiting to be filled. Mike's words were comforting. 'Listen, God is going to fill you. Don't have any doubts about that. Because God grants the desires of our hearts.'

Now it became a real issue in my life. I knew I couldn't go on without this baptism, and yet I also knew God wanted to give me this gift. Perhaps I was trying too hard? Receiving a gift surely isn't that difficult? I talked it through with God and told him that I wasn't going to struggle any more, just receive, and if he was going to keep his part of the bargain, this gift was mine.

In fact, it was the next Sunday that my insistence was rewarded. I went to Mike's church at Haringey, and while we were lost in worship with our hands stretched to heaven, it happened.

I saw a vision of Jesus on the cross. It was at the same time both horrific and beautiful, and I was deeply moved. I saw blood running down his side. I saw the agony of the Crucifixion, and yet I also saw the deep, inexplicable love that motivated it all. And I began to cry. As the tears rolled down my cheeks, I spoke out to the figure on the cross . . . and suddenly I realised I was not speaking in English, but in a strange language, and I knew I was being filled with the Holy Spirit at last.

Church service or not, I jumped up and down for joy. I let go and praised the Lord, jabbering away in the staccato language that God had given me, and Mike and some of the others around us rejoiced with me.

I felt great. My thirst was quenched, and yet I wanted more of this. I had been yearning for this for so long, but now I was filled. I was now a bold and effective witness, and I kissed goodbye to the fears that I had experienced while speaking for Jesus, never to accept them back again.

17: Black and white

With my twenty-third birthday came a pleasing sense of purpose in my life – the sort of feeling when you suddenly know for sure some of those things about God that have always been a mystery before. It was a growing security, and awareness that my life was important to God in working out his strategy. It was great to be alive!

The telephone rang. 'Is that Les Isaac?' The voice was confident, firm.

'Yeah, what can I do for you?'

The voice explained that a pentecostal church in Kentish Town was holding a special mission, and a projector was needed for a film show being arranged by the evangelist, a chap called Andrew Brandon. The name meant nothing to me at that moment, but it was a name that was soon to be very important to me.

The inquirer, a youth leader in the church, asked me if he could borrow our projector.

'Sure,' I said, pushing to the back of my mind any thoughts that it could get damaged in the wrong hands. 'I'll bring it round.'

I took the projector to the Kentish Town church on the following Friday night. On arrival I met the youth leader who was waiting with the evangelist. I shook hands with them, and took the projector inside.

'I'll show you how it works,' I announced. 'Which one of you will be operating it?'

There followed that comical moment when both looked to the other and said, 'He will.' We laughed.

'Well, I suppose I'll have to stay here and show the film for you,' I said. 'Where are the reels?'

They handed me two thirty-minute films, and I set about preparing the projector as young people began to drift in.

Andrew and the youth leader seemed to have everything under control, and when the building was full the lights went out and the film rolled.

Afterwards, Andrew preached a clear, concise gospel message, and I remember thinking how well-spoken he was, how English and yet not high-faluting or above the young people. He got through to them, and a number of them responded when he challenged them about the sincerity of their lives.

When the meeting was over, he came over and thanked me for showing the films for him.

'What do you do?' Andrew asked.

'Well, I show films a lot. Y'know, around youth clubs, churches, people's homes. Anywhere I can. And I preach the gospel anywhere and everywhere.'

We talked for about ten minutes. Then Andrew said, 'Why don't we meet and do something together?'

'Sounds good,' I said. 'I'll pray about that, and get in touch with you.'

About two months later – I had been snowed under with film-showing engagements – I went round to his house. I had telephoned and found out there was to be a small prayer meeting that evening, and when I arrived there were about half-a-dozen other people there.

When Andrew prayed he revealed that he had a strong burden for people living in the community in which he worked – Brent. I warmed to his sacrificial attitude, and I began to feel that there could be a partnership of some kind between us, working together for the Lord. I knew the Lord was trying to reveal something new to me, and after the others had left we talked about it and prayed together that God would make it perfectly clear what he wanted.

He was a little older than me – a steadying influence I thought – and white. I could see in my mind's eye the impact of a black–white partnership working together in London's immigrant areas. He was heavily built, well turned out, and had an attractive, warm-hearted wife.

So it wasn't long before we were planning a mission together for the Brent area. We approached all the churches in the area, and most of them agreed with us and were excited about the prospect of reaching the area for the Lord. There were Anglican, Pentecostal, Baptist, Moravian and Evangelical churches involved–quite a mixture which would have been impossible a few years previously. Now the prejudices were gone, and in their place was a common aim of working together in the kingdom of God.

The Anglican curate, Graham Kings, was a bundle of C of E dynamite. He was very keen, and backed the mission all the way. We planned gospel concerts with a group called Soulseekers, film shows and special rallies. The mission took the entire month of March 1980. We went into the youth clubs where we got a good reaction, and Andrew and I found ourselves preaching to crowds of eager and thoughtful kids.

The straight, no-holds-barred approach we adopted won many youths for the Lord, and it was not uncommon to see them break down and weep their way into the kingdom of God.

I really learned to let go in my preaching during that mission. Not that there was much self-consciousness in me anyway, but I discovered that the more I relaxed and trusted God the more his fire blazed in my life and his light flashed into the darkness like lightning. When I preached I felt as though the Holy Spirit was illuminating the loving figure of the Lord Jesus Christ, who had been hidden in a kind of dark gloom. I knew that these young people were seeing the Lord, not because of any skill in me and Andrew but because his raging fire was within us.

They didn't laugh at the way I waved my large, black hands around as I preached. They didn't snigger when I got excited and pranced around. They didn't mock when I kept repeating 'Hallelujah'. It was real, and they responded. That is the most thrilling thing about being a Christian: bringing others into the kingdom with you.

The mission was so effective that Andrew and I felt a bit like Paul and Silas on their missionary journeys in the book of Acts. We felt the success of the mission was a demonstration of God's approval of our partnership together, and we agreed to continue. God in his wisdom had identified a task that needed to be carried out and he had opened one door and let Andrew in, and then another door to let me in. Here we were at the threshold of an exciting new venture together, a venture that thrust the raw excitement of crew-fighting further down the dark, distant tunnel of the past, and which instead threw brilliant light on to the path for the future. I wouldn't have swopped this for anything!

18: Brixton

The Brandon–Isaac team became cemented in close friendship and a common calling. Andrew had a lot of experience in working in inner-city areas, but mainly with white Christians from all-white churches. I, too, had experience in London's urban areas, but mainly with black people. God, who sees no distinction, was now merging our ministries.

The Press began to notice this unusual teamwork, as did the periodical *Evangelism Today*. We were invited together to more and more places to hold missions or evangelistic meetings, and we were being plunged smack into the middle of God's plan for London. Eveywhere we went people were converted, and it was as we realised God's evident blessing on what we were doing that we set ourselves the goal of holding a mission in every London borough, especially where the churches were reluctant to go to the battle front. We wanted to reach everyone, and Rastas, skinheads and punks were foremost in our minds. They all had a need, regardless of whether they showed aggression or indifference, and that need could only be met in Jesus.

That year, evangelist Dick Saunders held a crusade in Brent and, after reading about us in *Evangelism Today*, invited us along. He asked me to testify in one meeting, with encouraging results. We again demonstrated to the world that we are one in Christ, whether black or white, and regardless of creed or culture. That was what God was saying to inner London. And we stood together to proclaim it.

At that time, tension was growing in Brixton. The scene was being set for the horrific riots of the summer of 1981 that would spark off violence in towns and cities all around the nation. Hate was brewing and, whenever we prayed, Andrew and I felt strangely drawn to that particular borough.

'Why don't we hold a mission there,' Andrew said one day. We could see a deep, deep need there, and we felt as though the Lord was leading us to Brixton.

We wrote to ministers, clergy and pastors in the area and explained our burden and our vision for the place, asking them to a meeting of Christian leaders. And all the signs we got were 'go', so we went!

Life was hard for me at that time. I was driving trucks for a transport firm all day, and I hardly had time to stop between finishing work and getting into Brixton to visit the youth clubs and set up the mission. Andrew, who worked full time in evangelism, spent the days going into schools and colleges. Our day ended in total exhaustion at eleven-thirty each night.

As we began to talk to people in the area, we found a mixed reception, with some people open to the gospel and some hostile. One evening we headed for a church in Vauxhall not far from the spot where we had been visiting some youth clubs. I knew there was a prayer meeting on at the church on Tuesday nights at seven p.m., and as we felt in need of prayer, we went. We were feeling a bit down in the mouth – the culmination of encountering rebuff and open aggression. People were suspicious of us, a white and a black man coming into their youth clubs, and we were getting the cold shoulder.

God knew about that. The prayer meeting hadn't been going long when a woman rose to her feet and prophesied. 'Be not dismayed or downcast,' she said in clear and authoritative tones. 'Be strong, for I am with you. Why should you be afraid when the Lord your God lives within you. I will strengthen you and I will uphold you as you look to me. Lean not to your own understanding, but draw upon me, for you cannot accomplish anything by your own strength, for it is not by might or by power but by my Spirit, says the Lord. I am with you.'

You can imagine what that did to us. The woman did not

know who we were, and probably didn't even know we were there anyway, but the Lord used her to speak his words of love and encouragement right into our lives there and then. We were so overjoyed and grateful that we caused a little bit of a commotion with our expressions of gratitude to the Lord. Now we could face anyone, and no task was too difficult or too daunting. Watch out Brixton!

After the prayer meeting, we talked to the pastor who told us he lived on what has become known as the 'frontline' – Railton Road. This is the street where hatred and tension seem to meet head-on, and if you walk along it you can sometimes sense the evil mood of aggression there. It is a road of collision and conflict. And that was where we wanted to go, especially after hearing so clearly from the Lord.

The pastor gave us directions to some youth clubs, and we climbed into Andrew's yellow Austin Allegro, not realising the similarity between his car and some of the vehicles the police were using in that area at that time. We were both dressed smartly, just like plain-clothed policemen might have looked.

Andrew followed the directions, and as we turned into Railton Road we were immediately confronted with a potentially explosive scene. There were about 200 people milling around in the street, and we decided to pull up and park the car without driving past the crowd. The air was heavy with tension, and we were uncertain of what was going on and what sort of reaction we would get if we approached the crowd.

We got out of the car. Immediately two elderly black men, in their fifties, came up to us.

'Here, you wanna buy some dope?'

'No thanks, we're Christians,' I replied. The two men didn't believe us, and looked at us with inquisitive yet threatening glances.

'Come on man,' and the drugs packet was thrust at us, menacingly.

Just then, a West Indian barely out of his teens came towards us snarling abuse and obscenities. He accused me of being an informer, a traitor to the brotherhood, and

Andrew, he decided, was a policeman. He left us in no doubt that if we had come to spy on what was going on, we weren't welcome, and there was a good deal of trouble in store for us.

Suddenly I noticed other people were beginning to stop and stare at us both, and I felt the tension heighten around us.

'Look man,' I began fearfully, although trying to conceal any trace of nervousness, 'we're Christians, and we are looking for some youth clubs. All we want to do is talk to some people about Jesus and start to arrange a mission here, that's all.'

The youth scowled and, although apparently unconvinced, he stepped aside. Andrew and I pushed through the drug dealers and the crowd and headed towards the spot where we thought there was a youth club.

Andrew, who had been the only white man in sight in Railton Road for the last few minutes–which had seemed like an eternity to us–muttered to me as we left the scene, 'If there was any time I felt a knife was going to be put in my back, it was then.'

We couldn't find the youth club. After half an hour of searching, we went back to Railton Road and headed towards the car. This time as we pushed through the crowd, which was still there, we saw one or two whites had arrived and they were being approached by the pushers just like we had been.

A voice behind us said, 'Did you find the club you were lookin' for?' It was the aggresive youth again. This time he seemed different, less angry, more open and talkative. We told him we hadn't been able to find the club.

He said, 'My name is Colin. Look, I'm sorry I swore at you like that, but I didn't believe what you were saying. I thought you were fuzz. But I can see you're different and maybe you're genuine. Please pray for me.' As we drove home that night, all I could hear echoing in my ears was, 'My name is Colin, pray for me.'

We realised there were people in desperate need in that place, people deep in sin, and some of them realised it. They would respond to the gospel, we knew now, thanks to

Colin. Even hard youths, their consciences seared by depravity, knew deep down that they needed the Lord. We both felt the weight of a yearning desire for the area to be won for Jesus, and we knew that the mission had begun.

Within a few weeks we were back in Railton Road, only this time we were approaching it with a different attitude. We spent a week going into houses, shops and clubs talking to people.

One door looked innocent enough, and it was opened by an elderly West Indian, shabbily dressed, his curly hair now a respectable wispy grey.

'Who you?' he asked in an agonisingly slow two-word question. His forehead wrinkled as his eyebrows raised to form the question-mark.

'We're Christians,' said Andrew. 'We've come to talk to you.'

The old man had been gazing at me, but now he lazily took his eyes from mine and looked blankly at Andrew. Then he once again drew his gaze back to me before slowly turning around giving a half-hearted 'follow me' wave with his left arm.

We followed. He led us painstakingly slowly up a narrow and creaking staircase, which in several places appeared to be rotting and about to collapse. At the top of three flights he pushed open a grimy unpainted door, to reveal a social meeting place. Two games of pool stopped, and every eye turned to peer through the smoky haze, darkened by lack of window light, to see who had arrived. The old man just wandered on in and picked up his drink leaving us to decide for ourselves what to do, so we gingerly stepped in after him.

There was a smell of take-away patties and hard dough bread, even a hint of rice and fish trying to assert itself above the strong smell of cigarette smoke and ganja.

The twenty or so people in the room remained silent for a few moments. Then one of the pool players mumbled through his cigarette that was still between his lips, 'Wot dem come here for?' And then he turned and continued his game.

We looked from eye to tye, and as we did so the men

returned one by one to the conversations, cards, drinking or whatever they had been doing before we arrived. But we knew that two things bothered them. We were strangers, and one of us was white.

Andrew moved first. He sauntered over to two men and introduced himself, feeling quite satisfied inside when they shook hands with him. Then the pool player spoke again, this time much more loudly, almost shouting.

'Tell white man to leave us alone.' He seemed to be appealing to Andrew and I to do something about the social standing of blacks in the area. 'Tell them to stop oppressin' us an' give us equality.' He paused for breath before saying the longer words 'oppressing' and 'equality', and overpronounced them in what seemed a comical way. But no one was going to laugh: this was a serious and desperate plea.

Andrew said, 'Do you realise the church did a lot to abolish slavery?' The pool player fixed his gaze firmly on Andrew, and appeared to calm down a little.

Andrew continued, 'Yes, we are aware Christianity has often gone wrong, and many have abused it. We know that if you see a man walking down the street with a collar on everyone thinks he is special but really he is not different from everyone else. A collar doesn't make him born again or even sincere in his beliefs.'

The man continued to look at Andrew, and others were now listening. 'The Bible says, you must be born again. Unless you give your life to Jesus, you can't be a Christian, because you can't be born again without confessing your sin and repenting from it.'

Then the pool player spoke again. 'If I had a machine gun,' he was speaking in a monotone voice this time, 'I would shoot all Christians starting with you two.'

I felt a shiver run down my spine as he spoke.

'Ministers, pfah,' he pretended to spit on the floor. 'They all behave bad, man, and all their churches are divided and angry.'

We talked with him some more, and eventually he agreed to let us pray with him, and I think we showed him a little bit of real Christianity, not pretend religion. Others listened while we talked, and by the time we left there seemed to be a general agreement with us, and we felt accepted by them.

Although we began to see a breakthrough in the conversations we were having with individuals in and around Brixton, when it came to holding meetings and concerts we weren't so successful. The whole area seemed to contain a spring-loaded sense of evil waiting to be hurled at us, and whenever we went into battle there we felt a bombardment of evil. More prayer was needed, and more awareness among the Christians in the area that they were involved in spiritual warfare, and if the evil 'strong man' who had a spiritual control over the region was to be plundered, he would first have to be bound and gagged by fervent prayer. Then people would be set free. And we were only just beginning to understand these things, and we were relatively inexperienced in them.

As the mission went on – or more accurately ground on – we felt as though we needed another fifty men. The task seemed too great for us. People were really searching but seemed not to find at that time. There were so many serious problems that gripped people's lives and held them captive, and a pall of evil hung over the area drawing it on towards the day when violence would erupt.

In the Brixton riots, Satan caused as much destruction and havoc as he could. He set people against people, not just police against youths. Between the two main riots, we talked with a youth leader from Railton Road who came to us with his feeling of desperation about what was going on. He seemed to be in the middle, trying unsuccessfully to calm things down. He despaired, and even though he wasn't a Christian he said, 'I honestly believe we need God in Brixton.' The task he took on himself of liaising between the people and the police was almost too much for him, and he nearly cracked up. And the violence that could still flare up in Brixton again will remain waiting in the wings no matter what political and social changes are made, until the area makes Jesus Christ, not Satan, its Lord.

19: Healing for Ealing

The calmness of the Reverend John Fulton seemed to bring an air of assurance to my living-room. He was curate of St James in Ealing and was there because he cared with every ounce of his being for the people in his parish. Now he was looking to Andrew and I to come into his area to reach those who seemed to have no interest in Christianity, and take the gospel right to the people who so desperately needed to hear it.

He sat there in his clerical collar and smart, dark suit, accepted a coffee from my wife Louise, and sat back in his chair. 'I've got a feeling this is the time for a breakthrough,' he announced in his unemotional voice.

I already knew that from the prayer he had just prayed while Louise was in the kitchen boiling the kettle. He had run one hand through his mousy hair, then clasped both hands together and shut his eyes tightly. Every word he spoke to his Father dripped compassion, and he had listed the dire tragedies he had encountered in his parish in a way that not only brought tears to my eyes but which also must have moved our heavenly Father.

Andrew and I had realised that we had before us a tremendous opportunity to reach inner-city areas, and we were overjoyed when we had been approached by this humble and honest minister. However, no other churches in Ealing seemed interested in coming in on this exciting adventure, so it appeared as though it was going to be a one-church crusade rather than multi-denominational. But Andrew and I had prayed about this mission, and if no other churches were going to chip in, well, we would carry on nevertheless and still expect great things to happen. And they did . . .

Andrew and I met with John and some of his workers at

St James. First we organised his flock into prayer cells to get the number one priority under way, and then we drew up lists of all the schools and youth clubs in the area. Then we organised home meetings for Christians to invite their friends along to friendly outreach evenings in an informal atmosphere.

The next day I found myself back at school. It was a strange feeling, having only just a few years previously left school, to be back and milling around with so many youngsters. Only this time they were behind the desks, and I was out in front. What a tremendous feeling of power!

Religious education lessons were still a bore, I found out. But the kids had heard a former Rasta was coming, and that brought a buzz of excitement to the school. A Rasta coming to talk about Jesus. Wow! Would he have locks? Would he pass around the ganja behind the bicycle shed? Would he bring a reggae band with him? These were the questions that ensured a full turn-out when I arrived.

On the way to the school that morning, Andrew had said, 'Les, you can't speak too much about the things you used to get up to at school, you'll give these kids bad ideas.'

I was glad he pointed that out, because it hadn't crossed my mind. Now I stood before these kids, and decided that the thing they needed to hear, and what I wanted to tell them, was how I met Jesus. So I told them, and they listened without any trace of boredom. Young people want reality and they can detect falseness of any kind.

As I went from class to class, I was inundated with eager questions from the kids who wanted to know what made me tick. In all, I only had time to visit two schools because I had to be at work, but Andrew visited more and found an eagerness and a hunger for spiritual things wherever he went.

In the two days I spent at schools, I quickly learned that the kids did not understand the language we Christians often used without thinking. Words like 'saved' and 'born again' were met with upstretched hands and the inquiry: 'What d'ya mean?' We discovered how important it was to think about what we were saying, to communicate carefully in words that could be easily understood, and not to lapse into the kind of jargon that evangelical and pentecostal Christians so often use.

In the evenings during those days prior to the mission actually starting, we visited youth clubs in the area. We would turn up at a club and mingle with the young people, talking to groups of them over a coffee and answering their quick-fire questions. Once some of these youths realised that we were genuine, and that God really had given us his power as we said he had, they began to ask us to pray for them. Many of them came from broken homes, and when they talked about their feelings we could see the sadness in their eyes, the hurt and pain left by the savage mauling life had given them. Others had nowhere to live, some had no friends and even no family, and many were in the depths of despair despite giving a cocky and confident outward appearance.

One evening a few of us went to a West Indian youth club. As we entered, I stood near the door for a moment to look around at the kids who were there. A few heads turned to take a look at the newcomers, but then they carried on with what they had been doing – playing table tennis, cards, just chatting, or taking in the loud reggae that was being played. Then I noticed one youth, and leaned back against the wall to study him for a moment or two.

He was fairly short, yet his manner made him seem taller than he was. He was brimming with confidence, always the central character, and clearly had quite a following. I made up my mind to go straight to him.

'Hey man, can I talk with you a minute?' The ring leader turned and looked at me straight in the eye as if expecting a confrontation or a challenge to his leadership, but when he looked he saw friendliness and visibly relaxed his guard.

'Sure. Wotcha want?'

'I'm a Christian,' I said, smiling, and immediately a few more heads turned to look at me. Our conversation was to have an audience. 'But I'm not a Bible-basher.' I felt I had to reassure them in case their defences went up again.

'OK, so what you doin' here then?' the ring leader asked.

'I want to tell you why I became a Christian, and also about a mission we're holding in the area.'

'Go on.'

That was an invitation you could not have kept me away from with a team of wild horses. 'I used to be a Rastafarian, but it didn't seem to make sense to me when Selassie died. Then I turned to Jesus, and he completely changed my life, because he's alive, man.' I really emphasised the word 'alive', drawing the sharp and dramatic contrast between the central figures of the two faiths. One dead, the other risen from the dead. I went on to explain to the ring leader, and of course everyone else in earshot, just how I came to the point where I discovered the truth, how I gave my life to Christ, and what it meant to me now. And they listened.

When I had finished the ring leader spoke. 'Look, man, I used to go to church, y'know. I used to go to church when I was a boy. But now I'm over that.' He explained how he had turned to Selassie and Rastafarianism, but then made an astonishing admission that made me realise he was ready to become a Christian.

'People used to tell me Selassie was King of kings. Every week someone would sell me a big picture of Selassie, costin' me about £10, an' I took them home and put them on my wall where I could look at them. But the more I look at dem, I realise Selassie was jus' a man. I realise that 'im dead, man. All men has to die, Selassie too.'

He was now beginning to open up, and there were some looks of intrigue on the faces of some of his followers. He turned to one of them.

'Hey, man, can you see Selassie?'

'No, man,' said the startled youth, after just a moment's hesitation to decide whether it was a trick question or not.

'See, you can't see 'im, because he's dead.' The startled youth nodded, thankful that he had passed the test and got his answer right.

Then the ring leader's face went deadly serious, and he turned to me with a look on his face that said he was now speaking about a deep and meaningful part of his life that he was gently opening up after years of it remaining firmly shut.

'Look, I'm goin' to be truthful,' he said. 'One day I'm goin' to become a Christian. But not right now 'cos I rebel.

But one day I'm goin' to become like you an' preach the gospel because Jesus is the only way and I don't believe in Selassie now.'

I put my arm around him – probably the first West Indian man to have dared to do that with this ring leader for some years – and although he was a little embarrassed, I silently let him know that I knew he meant what he had said. We talked on for a while, and then suddenly he announced he was taking me to meet someone.

We walked for about ten minutes to a nearby café where he introduced me to a Rastafarian – tall, dark and with very long dreadlocks. We talked about Christianity but now the conversation became very weighted against white people because this Rasta was bitter. I prayed with them both there and then in the café, and told them about the mission, and they both said they would come.

The next evening I went to a youth club that was totally different from the West Indian club. It had a reputation of being frequented by young members of the National Front! Even the thought of a West Indian waltzing into a place like that didn't put me off, because when it came down to hard facts, these were kids who were human and who needed the Lord, and that was all that mattered. So I went there with a friend from St James's Church.

When we arrived we were met by the youth leader who was clearly interested to see how this would go down. With a gesture, he said 'Carry on' and left us to do whatever we wanted.

I looked around. All the kids were white, except, surprisingly, two half-caste youths, and a black girl. As we entered, just about every head turned to stare at me with accusing eyes. I decided to take the bull by the horns, and walked up to the nearest group of skinheads and said, 'Hey, wotcha think about Christianity?' It seemed a stupid question to be asking, but I couldn't think of any other way of starting a conversation.

One of the skinheads said, 'Well, we don't go to church and we don't believe in it.'

So I said, 'I used to be a skinhead.' They seemed to take a second, more detailed, look at me when I said that. 'Yeah, I used to go around in my blue staypresses, Ben Sherman, loafers and so on. I used to go around givin' guys a kickin', I used to be in crew-fights . . .' I felt as though I was getting a strange respect using language like that. I let them know I knew what they were on about, and that I understood their language.

I had the interest of some of them, but others were only looking for a laugh. They were making obscene comments and spitting on the floor as I spoke, but I ignored their filthy manners.

Of the group that seemed to be interested, there was one youth who was obviously set apart in some way as their leader. He motioned the others to keep quiet and listen. They did. I had their attention for about twenty minutes as I spoke about how running the streets had got to the point where I felt empty and unfulfilled, how I turned to Selassie and still felt empty, and how I then found Jesus and was filled at last.

When I finished, one of them said, 'You say you are a Christian. What would you do if you were walking down the road and some skins came up to you and called you a nigger and was gettin' aggressive. What would you do?'

I thought for a moment, silently lifting my mind to God for the kind of wisdom Jesus always showed when he answered awkward questions, and said, 'A lot of people appear to be very aggressive and they have a front, but deep down they are scared. Most are only tough when their friends are there, but on their own they are chicken, cowards. I believe tht if you show these kind of kids that you're not scared, they back off, and I would show them I'm not scared because I have Someone inside me who's bigger, tougher and stronger than any skinhead. An' he's never let me down yet.

'I would tell 'em three things. One, I'm a nigger and there's nothin' you or I can do about that. Two, if you can give me one good reason why you should hate me, I will say, 'hate on, man'. Three, God loves everyone, and there's no black or white in the kingdom of God, just God's people.'

The youth who asked the question seemed quite impressed

with my answer, and I silently lifted a grateful heart to God for the answer he had put in my mouth. Then I added, 'I saw Asians beaten up, I used to do it myself. I saw them beaten up for money, or for a laugh. But just to beat up someone because you hate the colour of his skin is not only totally wrong, it is totally dumb.'

The way I said 'dumb' immediately made those who had put the boot into Pakistanis and Indians, just because they were Asians, feel very small, and I saw some of them look down with shifty eyes, ashamed and embarrassed, and hopefully changed.

The next question was why people starve, if there's a God.

'Greed,' I said. 'One of man's basic problems, and yours too if you're honest. There's enough to go round everyone if we give.'

They asked how to become Christians, and I told them what happened to me. They thought it was something dramatic, but I assured them it was the simplest thing a man or a woman could do, but only if they had a sincere heart. The number of youths who crushed around us grew and grew as I told them that Jesus had said he would not hinder anyone who came to him. We didn't have to seek out individuals – they came to us with searching questions and a genuine hunger for God.

We told them about the concert we were holding that week with a group called Paradise, but their first question was, 'Are there going to be niggers there who want to give us trouble?'

'There won't be no trouble,' I told them, and I could see their faces register assurance.

When Andrew and I arrived for the concert we surveyed the scene that was the result of several days' hard work. It was full, with schoolchildren and kids in the front rows, some of them with their parents. In the back left-hand corner as we looked from the stage were a large number of skinheads from the last club I had visited, laughing and joking among themselves with their Dr Martins boots on the chairs in front. In the other corner at the back were black youths and a few rude boys.

One of the skinheads called me over. He was glad to see me, but I could sense a hint of apprehension about him. 'Those niggers are lookin' at us,' he said, seemingly unconcerned at addressing a West Indian with that term. It was as if he no longer considered me as of another race. 'There might be a fight.'

Some of these youths had been fighting not long ago in the area, and the skinhead's fears were justified. But I told him, 'Don't worry, if you don't cause any trouble everything will be all right,' and I know I spoke from faith that trusted the God who had set all this up to look after details like that.

The music was good. Paradise put in all the ingredients to attract the attention of coloured youths and skinheads alike, with good reggae rhythms mixed with excellent jazz-funk. The gospel came over clearly, both in the lyrics and in the testimonies between songs, and the whole audience seemed to be enjoying it. They were thinking, 'Can this really be Christianity, where you can enjoy yourself with good music?'

Sadly, about half of the skinheads filed out about half-way through, seemingly unable to sit still and take in what was going on for more than an hour or so. But some stayed put, including the leader of the pack and the ones with him who had shown more interest.

When the band stopped playing, I stepped on to the stage to speak for a few moments. I looked out into the audience, and thought how only a few years previously I might have been one of those faces. I stood still for a moment in deep gratitude to God for what he had done for me, and silently lifting my heart to him to ask for wisdom, power and love to shine through me at this moment.

'The gospel is very simple,' I began. 'God's own Son, Jesus, gave up all the splendour of heaven and came right down into this mess-up of a world and died for the likes of you and me. He took all your sin on himself, and he died in your place. For all those evil things you have done, for those kickings you have given each other and given to innocent people, and for all the wrong that you know is in your lives – he died.'

I challenged them without mincing my words, and laid the gospel on the line. The choice was theirs. Either they accepted Christ and his forgiveness, or they walked out of that theatre having completely and wilfully rejected his love and his undoubted claims on their lives.

As I drew my talk to a conclusion, I said, 'All over this audience God has been speaking to people. He loves you, and wants to help you, and give you his life. As this concert ends, if you want to become a Christian, or if you want us to pray with you, come down to the front and we will be here to help you.'

Andrew and I waited down at the front, and at first no one moved. It was as if everyone was waiting to see who would go down to the front first. Then a group of girls came down to the front, and that was the signal for more to come. More than thirty youths came forward to give their lives to Christ or to be counselled, including two of the skinheads. I prayed with them both, and later one of them was converted while the other was followed up by the church's curate.

That night God had moved in power and spoken to kids off the street right where they were. They had responded and proved that God is true to his word: 'When you seek me you will find me'. And for me, it was the first encouraging step towards the revival that God is now beginning among skinheads, Rastas and various rude boys in London. People who need Jesus . . . and who will find him.

20: The vision

We've read about great men of God like Finney, Moody and Wesley. We've all heard about great revivals abroad and in this country where people have been on their knees seeking God, where pubs have been forced to close because everyone was too busy praying to have time for social drinking.

But my aim is to see a real move of God's Holy Spirit today, and a fresh move of the Spirit that is unique and even greater than anything anyone has ever experienced before. The Church coming really alive, and forgetting differences of opinion on doctrine or style of worship, just being joyfully taken up with God and motivated by the simple aim of telling people about Jesus. The people of God knowing and experiencing the fullness of the power of God. That's what I want to see.

This is my threefold vision:

1. To make sure the whole of London hears the gospel.
2. To see thousands, millions saved and filled with the Holy Spirit.
3. To see a steady rise in various ministries to build up the Church.

My job is evangelism. That is what God has called me to do, and that is what he has equipped me to do. That means I not only want to tell as many people as possible about my Jesus, but I want to pass on my gift to other people so they can tell people too. Ephesians 4. 12 says gifts like mine are given by God 'to equip the saints for the work of ministry, for building up the body of Christ.'

A lot of Christians might have the attitude, 'Les Isaac is doing a great job'. But that's not what it's all about. If everyone did what God wants them to do, go out and start living in the real world for Jesus and stop living in a dream world, this country would be transformed. More Christians need to realise God just wants them to live for him in their community and let his power work through them. Not to get under pressure or feel guilty, but just to be aware that if they speak his word or minister in his name, fantastic things will happen because the Holy Spirit is the greatest and strongest power in the whole of creation and that power is in us! We all have homes, school or work where we can let Jesus be seen.

When I was at school there was a Christian there who, it turned out, was scared to talk to me. I don't blame him for that, because I wasn't the most trustworthy of characters. But little did he know that if he had plucked up courage and told me about Jesus I would probably have been converted on the spot!

If today's Church gets its priorities right like the early Church did in the book of Acts, God is going to move. There will be no stopping him, because although Satan will try to mess it up, he is a defeated foe. Jesus said, 'I *will* build my church, and the gates of hell shall not prevail against it.'

I have no difficulty in believing that the majority in a city like London can be Christian – not nominally Christian, but Spirit-filled. That is my vision. The faith God has given me believes it. And I expect it . . .

Appendix 1: Rastafarianism

There's no mistaking Rastafarians. They are so conspicuous with their long, flowing 'dreadlocks', the mark of a brotherhood cult that has been formed by and for social outcasts.

Rastafarianism is a way of life to the Rasta, and much more than a set of religious beliefs. It offers answers to life's complex problems faced by black people, and gives a re-sili-ence in the face of oppressive poverty and the dire struggle of everyday living. It is inspiration to the Rasta, often giving rise to music, particularly reggae, and other art forms.

The roots of Rastafarianism

In 1444 Christopher Columbus sailed into the scenic Discovery Bay, Jamaica. He found an island inhabited by native Arawak Indians, but after his discovery it fast became populated with Africans. The white slave-traders took vast numbers of Africn tribespeople to the West Indies and the American mainland, and in so doing laid the foundations of Rastafarianism.

Slavery naturally bred discontent and resistance into a strong-willed people. It was a subdued resistance, because stringent and horrifying penalties had to be paid by slaves for insubordination or attempted escape, but it was, none the less, an aggressive aspect being steadily built into the Africans forcibly taken from their homeland.

The fading memories of their beloved Africa were recorded for posterity in their ritualistic songs and dances, and always there was a thread running through West Indian culture that the white man had stolen them from their homeland across the sea. Thus they remembered the freedom of the African bush, and thus the resentment grew and grew.

Beautiful and pleasant though the Caribbean was, the slaves' imprisonment made it unbearable for most. The great dream was somehow to cross the vast ocean and go home to Africa, literally a physical impossibility for any slave who was bound to his master's farm for life and perpetually penniless. And the more the white land-owners repressed and punished their slaves, the stronger the desires grew to go home.

Thus in Jamaica there were only two types of people. The white and the black. The rich and the poor. The free and the slave. The happy and the sad. The lords and the oppressed.

Marcus Garvey

In 1887 Marcus Garvey was born in St Anns Bay, Jamaica, the youngest of eleven children born to a very poor couple.

Although he was educated with white children, as a teenager Garvey became acutely aware that in the eyes of the world in which he lived the Negro was inferior. He saw the social differences, the separation and the racism, and it stung his soul deeply.

As a young man, Garvey became in effect the first black freedom-fighter, and as such soon had a following. He became something of a hero, and was admired by many Jamaicans. He gained support in his stand for freedom by using biblical quotations to give weight to his message, striking home in the hearts of thousands of black Jamaicans who clung to Christian doctrine.

In the 1920s he founded the ill-fated Universal Negro Improvement Association, which he set up to encourage Jamaicans to return to Africa. But the crucial connection between Garvey and Rastafarianism can be traced to his prophecy when he said, 'Look to Africa when a black king shall be crowned, for the day of deliverance is near.'

Interest in Garvey, however, waned as no clear signs of an end to the Jamaicans' social inferiority resulted, and he retreated to England as a forgotten man.

But when Ras Tafari ('Prince Tafari'), who claimed to be

a direct descendant of King Solomon and the Queen of Sheba, was crowned Emperor Haile Selassie of Ethiopia in 1930, people took notice. And it was not insignificant that titles such as 'Lord of lords,' 'King of kings' and 'Conquering Lion of Judah' were given to him at his coronation.

Garvey's message came back to life as a result of his prophecy coming true. His philosophy of self-redemption for black people, return to Africa, racial purity and the spiritual brotherhood of black people, was again on the increase. And since his death in England in 1940, Garvey has been seen as the prophet and inspirer of the Rastafarian movement, the John the Baptist of the new faith.

Rasta life in Jamaica

The first Rastafarians appeared in Jamaica in 1930 after Ras Tafari's coronation. Jamaicans began to search the Bible, and took great comfort in their suffering from the words written for persecuted early Christians. Some saw the book of Revelation as a direct message to the oppressed black nations about their suffering and read into it the messiahship of Haile Selassie, quoting texts like Revelation 19. 16 'On his robe and on his thigh he has a name inscribed, King of kings and Lord of lords.'

The basic beliefs of Rastafarians that began to take firm hold at this time were the divinity of Haile Selassie, the certainty that white society would collapse, and the promise of a return to the African homeland for all descendants of slaves. The 'Babylon' of the book of Revelation was interpreted as white man's civilization and society.

It caught on because West Indians wanted something to grasp and cling on to, they wanted hope and brotherhood. Many of them were moving from island to island in the Caribbean searching for work and a home, and economic depression was putting a pall of gloom over the West Indies. The concept of an African destiny gripped their imagination.

Among the things Garvey spoke of was the great departure

for Africa. He had given 1960 as the year by which West Indians would be home, and on many occasions just prior to that up to 15,000 people turned up at Kingston, Jamaica, having bought bogus tickets for trips to their homeland. The ships they queued for never came.

Rasta teaching

The divinity of Selassie. The phrases that Ras Tafari used when he was crowned emperor gave rise to this doctrine. He claimed to be a direct descendant of King David, and therefore the scripture in Revelation 5. 2–5 ('Behold, the Lion of the tribe of Judah, the root of David, hath prevailed') became the basis of teaching that Selassie was redeemer for Rastas.

After his coronation, the acceptance of Selassie as the living God increased and simultaneously there was a frantic search of the Scriptures for a basis for this. Any passage of the Bible sufficed if it lent weight to the doctrine, but the main ones used were Isaiah 43. 1–5 and 24–28; Ezekiel 37. 19–25 and Revelation 1. 14 and 17–18.

Rastafarianism states that the spirit of Ras Tafari is universal and eternal, thus getting round the problem of his death in 1975 which has not diminished Rasta faith in his divinity.

The collapse of white society. Race is a big issue for Rastas, and one central issue in their faith is the certainty of the coming ruin of 'Babylon' – white society and its allies. To the Rasta, whites are the oppressors and the allies of Satan. Blacks, on the other hand, are seen as 'God's chosen people', although this does not mean that all black people are included in the special race. Many are 'lost sinners', those who help white society in any way.

The return. Rastas have a hope, in both a spiritual and a physical sense, of a return to Africa. The spiritual aspect of this is the regaining of the dignity of their forefathers which was robbed when they were enslaved. They have a deep, inner search for the reality of who they are and where they are going. Most Rastas believe they are reversing the process that took place with slavery by their diet, dress, hair style, speech, political and spiritual beliefs.

But they are also looking to return physically to Africa, not just to African ways. And in particular, many want to go to Ethiopia. There is a parallel here with the Christian expectation of heaven and eternal life. Some Rastas have a stronger hope of a literal return to Africa, others major on the spiritual aspect of living, but either way, Africa plays an important part in the Rasta's life.

Other beliefs. Doctrine, for the Rasta, is somewhat loose. There are no firm rules for beliefs, but among Rastas there are those who believe the following: God, Jesus and the early Christians were blacks; Haile Selassie is now living in another dimension; whites are 'devils'; Rastafarians are the true Jews. Some also believe in reincarnation, and claim to have 'relived' horrific journeys on slave trading ships.

Ganja

Smoking ganja (marijuana) is a common practice of Rastafarians. It is seen as being important to spiritual, mental and physical health, and its scriptural backing is said to be Genesis 1. 11–12 where all plants are called 'good' by God. Ganja is of course outlawed in many societies, including Britain, and one Rastafarian leader had said this is because 'Babylon' is afraid that smoking ganja will lead people to the truth.

Individual Rastas smoke ganja in what is called a 'spliff' (hand-rolled cigarette), and groups smoke together with what is called a 'Chalise pipe', passing it from one to the other.

Dreadlocks

The meaning behind this description of a Rastafarian's long

braids is that people fear the black man with locks, hence the term *dread*locks.

Locks are formed simply by allowing the hair to grow, washing it and allowing it to dry without brushing it or treating it. Some actually plait it, but for most Rastas the simplicity of long, untreated hair is a throwback to Africa.

A Rasta's locks are also a symbol of holiness and his devotion to the Rastafarian faith. The longer the better. Therefore, cutting his locks is unthinkable.

British Rastafarianism

The Rasta in Jamaica is different from his brothers in Britain. European influence has inevitably affected the cult; for instance, it is a predominantly white and therefore hostile society.

Rastafarianism has therefore caught on rapidly among black youths in Britain, often fanned by hostile parents who cannot come to terms with its beliefs. The crisis of conflict in an angry society has for many West Indian youths come at a time of searching for peace and spiritual reality.

More devoted Rastas in Britain have formed church groups – in this respect they are behind their Jamaican counterparts – and they often rally together in large numbers to celebrate certain feast days and functions.

Appendix 2: Reaching out to Rastas

If you are a Christian, love the Lord Jesus with all your heart, and are filled with his power, love and wisdom, then you can share the life of Christ with Rastas just as you can with anyone else. You don't have to be a former drug addict to bring a hippy to the Lord, or be a millionaire to lead a wealthy person to Jesus.

It is important to approach Rastas with confidence because they are quick to take the upper hand and appear cocky even though they may not be sure what they actually believe. Remember, in Christ you have the truth, so don't be ashamed of his gospel or reticent in presenting it. And it is also vital to remember that Jesus loves Rastas much more than you do, so let his love motivate you.

Starting point

Some Rastafarians are just passing through the cult as if in a transitory stage. They are on a journey and expecting to move on, and some may not even admit this but you can sense they are not deeply entrenched in Rasta beliefs.

Some, however, have turned to Rastafarianism to fulfil a deep need, often inseparably linked with a mistrust of white people. They genuinely see their brotherhood as much deeper than skin colour or lifestyle, and are entombed in the cult.

There are some, though, who have had some experinece of Christianity, often through religious West Indian parents who have forced them to attend church all through their childhood. While these Rastas are unlikely to have had a genuine conversion to Christianity of their own, they have heard the gospel preached over and over again, and they know what you are talking about. These Rastas are very often the hardest of the lot to reach, and they are a sorry testimony to well-intentioned but foolish upbringing that seeks to dominate a child. Children and young people need to be led and encouraged into reality, not pushed, and there are many Rastas who are living proof that being made to go to church doesn't make you a Christian.

But Jesus loves each one with a perfect love, and wants to reach out to them in just the same way as he reached out to Zacchaeus or Peter.

Diversity

It is important to remember that not all Rastas believe the same thing. Sometimes the only thing that is common between Rastas is their locks, and it would be a mistake to assume there is a consensus of belief among them.

Therefore, when you talk to a Rasta, try to find out immediately where he stands. Don't assume he automatically believes Haile Selassie is divine, for instance. Be ready to take a different line of approach for different Rastas – there are no stock answers.

Common ground

Christians and Rastas have a common respect for the Bible, and in the case of the latter it is the King James authorized version. So if you don't feel you are being accepted in your opening remarks, focus attention on the Bible for a moment and there you should find common ground.

When you look into the Bible, you will find there common recognition. For instance, God. You both recognise the same God, the creator of heaven and earth (Genesis) and the Word who made everything (John 1).

Also in the Bible, you will find the same sin referred to by both faiths. 'The wages of sin is death,' says Romans 6. 23. With that scripture in mind you can tell them that when Israel sinned, they were punished by God if they did not repent after he had pleaded with them to return to him (Judges 3. 7–8; 6. 1; 13. 1 etc.). Man is inherently evil. That is not hard to prove, even for the Rastafarian who is looking to Africa – for there some African tribes hate each other and kill, maim and destroy one another.

In the Bible, too, you will find the same separation that is caused by sin. 'All have sinned and come short of the glory of God' (Romans 3. 23) and that means living death (Romans 6. 23). Adam was the first to discover that separation, and no one since has been exempt from it. Everyone, Rastafarians included, becomes aware of their need for God at some point.

Reunion not repatriation

Many Rastas are looking to Africa, and pinning all their hope and faith in going back to the continent of their roots. To them, Africa is a kind of heaven.

But the Rasta needs to know that God is looking for reunion not repatriation. He has made a way to restore fellowship between himself and man, and the Rastafarian's longing for Africa is just a misguided substitute for the 'longing for heaven' that many Christians experience. The irrepressible desire to be with God.

The Rasta that goes 'home' to Africa is a disillusioned and empty person. The realisation of his dream has not proved to be the answer. Try to show the Rasta you talk to that Jesus fully satisfies. He fills you up with his love. It is spiritual and not physical or geographical. Only forgiveness of sin 'takes' anyone to God, through Jesus.

The Christian's destination is heaven. That's better than Africa! No flies, no extreme heat, no fierce animals. Instead streets of gold and, above all, Jesus! Heaven is the only place where government works, perfectly, and without a hitch, totally opposite to Africa – the land of *coups*, political murder, apartheid and rioting.

Man or saviour?

Jesus died for the world's sins, and rose again. Selassie died. He is still dead. And anyway, he once professed that Christ is the only way to God. There's no argument about facts like a man's death, yet Rastafarianism has survived Selassie's demise. But neither is there any tangible proof that Jesus is alive *now*, except the proof we know for ourselves in our hearts. People manage to explain everything away that we know to be true, but the fact is *we know*, and calm assurance is the best way to demonstrate that knowledge, not arrogant dogmatism.

Technique

Don't argue with Rastas, they're not always rational. His word is 'reasoning' and he loves to discuss spiritual things. So present the facts, the truth, and let God do the convincing.

Keep the pace of your conversation slow. Don't get worked up, and try not to race ahead with ideas and arguments. Avoid confusion by taking things easy and dealing with facts one by one.

Don't worry if your words do not seem to be having any immediate effect. The Rasta you are speaking to may not appear to have heard you, but many converted Rastas have testified that they remember the words of Christians who spoke to them.

Pray for the Rasta you talk to. Don't assume that witnessing on its own is enough, but be prepared to wrestle in prayer for him. Satan is not going to let go of anyone easily, and there may well be a need for intercession and spiritual warfare.

Jesus has 'disarmed' all demons and satanic powers (Colossians 2. 15), so don't be afraid to speak out loud while you are praying on your own to remind the evil one of what Jesus has done. He hates that! And then command those satanic powers to release the one for whom you are praying. Fast as well as pray if you feel led by God to do so.

When a Rasta is brought to the Lord, it is vital to ensure that he or she is encouraged to go on with the Lord. Every new Christian needs to be in a loving, caring New Testament church, to be personally trained and built up by a strong Christian, to be baptised in water, to receive the Holy Spirit, and to be soundly taught the Scriptures.

There's plenty to do – get cracking!

Scriptures

Get your Bible and follow these scriptures through; they will be a great help as you witness to Rastas: Deuteronomy 18. 15; Isaiah 9. 6; Isaiah 53. 1–12; Matthew 1. 1–25; Luke 2. 1–54; Matthew 11. 28–30; Matthew 17. 1–8; John 5. 1–47; John 10. 1–42; (especially vv. 7–10); Hebrews 1–8 (especially 7. 23–28); Hebrews 10. 3–7; Matthew 16. 15–16; Acts 4. 12; 1 Timothy 2. 3–6; Revelation 22. 6–21.